Spanish Medical Dictionary

Spanish-English English-Spanish

Introduction

This book contains essential information that will help medical professionals, health workers, and students break the language and cultural barriers between Spanish and English speakers and enable them to provide quality care to their patients. It provides precise translations for the most commonly used terms in the field of medicine and health care. It features translations for dialogues, phrases, instructions, unit conversions, abbreviations, and other important health concerns.

Table of contents

Chapter 1 - Conversions and Medical Abbreviations

Volumen/Capacidad (Volume/Capacity)

1 mililitro (milliliter)	0.034 onzas fluidas (fluid ounces)
1 mililitro (milliliter)	0.2 cucharaditas (teaspoons)
1 onza fluida (fluid ounce)	29.6 mililitros (milliliters)
1 cucharadita (teaspoon)	4.93 mililitros (milliliters)
1 taza (cup)	0.24 litros (liters)
1 cuarto (quart)	0.95 litros (liters)
1 litro (liter)	4.227 tazas (cups)
1 litro (liter)	1.057 cuartos (quarts)
1 litro (liter)	0.264 galones (gallons)
1 galón (gallon)	3.785 litros (liters)
1 cucharada (tablespoon)	3 cucharadita (teaspoons)
1 onza fluida (fluid ounce)	2 cucharada (tablespoons)
1 medio litro (pint)	16 onza fluidas (fluid ounces)

Longitud (Length)

1 centímetro (centimeter)	0.3937 pulgadas (inches)
1 pulgada (inch)	2.54 centímetros (centimeters)
1 pie (foot)	30.48 centímetros (centimeters)
1 pie (foot)	0.3048 metros (meters)
1 yarda (yard)	0.9144 metros (meters)
1 metro (meter)	1.093613 yardas (yards)
1 metro (meter)	1.093613 yardas (yards)
1 kilómetro (kilometer)	0.621 millas (miles)
1 milla (mile)	1.609344 kilómetros (kilometers)

Peso (Weight)

1 gramo(gram)	0.353 onzas ounces
1 onza (ounce)	28.35 gramos(grams)
1 kilogramo (kilogram)	2.2046 libras (pounds)
1 libra (pound)	453.6 gramos (grams)
1 libra (pound)	0.4563 kilogramos (kilograms)
1 tonelada (ton)	0.907 toneladas métricas

Medical Abbreviations

AA   Alcohólicos Anónimos   AA – Alcoholics Anonymous
AMA   arco de movilidad articular   range of motion
CRG   coronariografía   coronary angiogram
ECV   enfermedad cerebrovascular   cerebrovascular disease
EPOC   Enfermedad pulmonar obstructiva crónica   COPD
SNC   sistema nervioso central   central nervous system
SSN   solución salina normal   normal saline solution
RAO   Retención aguda de Orina   acute urinary retention
TGP   transaminasa glutámico pirúvico   glutamic pyruvic transaminase
ERC   enfermedad renal crónica   chronic kidney disease
ICC   insuficiència cardíaca congestive   chronic heart failure
SIV   septum interventricular   interventricular septum
SIDA   Síndrome de Inmunodeficiencia Adquirida   AIDS
FRCV   factor de riesgo cardiovascular   cardiovascular risk factor
SDR   Síndrome de distrés respiratorio   respiratory distress syndrome
PAM   presión arterial media   median blood pressure
ECC   enfermedad cardíaca crónica   chronic heart disease
VIH   virus de inmunodeficiencia humana   HIV – Human Immunodeficiency Virus
TAC   tomografía axial computarizada   CAT scan

Chapter 2   - Anatomy

El Cuerpo Humano (The Human Body)

el abdomen	abdomen
el antebrazo	forearm
la axial	armpit
la barbilla	chin
la boca	mouth
el brazo	arm
la cadera	hip
la cara	face
la cintura	waist
el codo	elbow
el cráneo	skull
el cuello	neck
el dedo del pie	toe
el escroto	scrotum
la espalda	back
la frente	forehead
el hombre	shoulder
la ingle	groin
la mano	hand
la manzana de Adán	Adam's apple
el mentón	chin
la muñeca	wrist
el muslo	thigh
las nalgas	buttocks
la nuca	nape
el ojo	eye
el ombligo	navel
el omóplato	shoulder blade

la oreja	ear (outer)
la pantorrilla	calf
la parte superior del brazo	upper arm
el pecho	chest
el pelo	hair
el pene	penis
el pezón	nipple
el pie	foot
la pierna	leg
el pliegue anal	posterior rugae
el pubis	pubis
la región lumbar	loin
la rodilla	knee
el seno	breast
la sien	temple
el sobaco	armpit
el talon	heel
el tobillo	ankle
el tórax	thorax
el tronco	trunk
la vulva	vulva

La Cabeza (The Head)

la barba	beard
la barbilla	chin
el bigote	moustache
la boca	mouth
el cabello	hair
el cachete	cheek
la cara	face
la ceja	eyebrow
el cuello	neck

el cutis	skin, facial complexion
el diente	tooth
la fosa nasal	nostril
la frente	forehead
el hoyuelo	dimple
el labio	lip
la lengua	tongue
la mandíbula	jaw
la mejilla	cheek
el mentón	chin
el mostacho	moustache
la nariz	nose
el ojo	eye
la oreja	ear (outer)
el párpado	eyelid
la partidura	part
la patilla	sideburn
el pelo	hair
la pestaña	eyelash
la piel	skin, facial complexion
el pómulo	cheekbone
la raya	part
la sien	temple

Los Órganos Internos (Internal Organs)

el apéndice vermicular	appendix
la arteria	artery
el bazo	spleen
el cerebro	brain
el corazón	heart
el esófago	esophagus
la espina dorsal	spinal cord

el estómago	stomach
la garganta	throat
el hígado	liver
los intestinos	intestines
el músculo	muscle
el páncreas	pancreas
la piel	skin
el pulmón	lung
el riñón	kidney
la tráquea	windpipe
la vejiga	bladder
la vena	vein
la vesícula biliar	gall bladder

El Sistema Reproductor Femenino (Female Reproductive System)

la ampolla de la trompa uterina	ampulla of fallopian/uterine tube
la areola	areola
la citoplasma	cytoplasm
el clítoris	clitoris
el conducto galactófero	lactiferous duct
la corona radiata	corona radiate
el cuello del útero	cervix of uterus
el pabellón de la trompa de Falopio	infundibulum of fallopian tube
la glándula mamaria	mammary gland
el huevo	egg
el istmo de la trompa de Falopio	isthmus of fallopian tube
el labio mayor	labium majus
el labio menor	labium minus

el ligamento ancho del útero	broad ligament of uterus
el ligamento redondo del útero	round ligament of uterus
el monte de Venus	mons pubis
el núcleo	nucleus
el nucléolo	nucleolus
el ovario	ovary
el pezón	nipple
el saco de Douglas	pouch of Douglas
el saco uterovesical	uterovesical pouch
el seno	breast
el tejido adiposo	adipose tissue
la trompa de Falopio	fallopian tube
la uretra	urethra
el útero	uterus
la vagina	vagina
la vejiga	urinary bladder
la vulva	vulva
la zona pelúcida	zona pellucida

El Sistema Reproductor Masculino (Male Reproductive System)

el conducto deferente	deferent duct
el conducto eyaculador	ejaculatory duct
el cordón espermático	spermatic cord
el cuerpo cavernoso	cavernous body
el cuerpo esponjoso de la uretra	bulbocavernous muscle
el escroto	scrotum
el espermatozoide	spermatozoon
el glande	glans penis

la glándula de Cowper	Cowper's gland
el meato urinario	urinary meatus
el pene	penis
el prepucio	prepuce
la próstata	prostate
el testículo	testicle
la uretra	male urethra
la vejiga	urinary bladder
la vesícula seminal	seminal vesicle

El Sistema Respiratorio (Respiratory System)

la aorta	aorta
el diafragma	diaphragm
el bronquio derecho	right bronchus
el bronquiolo terminal	terminal bronchiole
el corazón	heart
el esófago	esophagus
el lóbulo inferior	lower lobe
el lóbulo medio	middle lobe
el lóbulo superior	upper lobe
el pericardio	pericardium
el pulmón derecho	right lung
el pulmón izquierdo	left lung
la epiglottis	epiglottis
la arteria pulmonary	pulmonary artery
la cavidad bucal	oral cavity
la cavidad nasal	nasal cavity
la cavidad pleural	pleural cavity
la cuerda vocal	vocal cord
la faringe	pharynx
la laringe	larynx
la pleura parietal	parietal pleura

la tráquea	trachea
la vena cava superior	superior vena cava

El Sistema Urinario (Urinary System)

la aorta abdominal	abdominal aorta
la arteria ilíaca común	common iliac artery
la arteria ilíaca interna	internal iliac artery
la arteria mesentérica inferior	inferior mesenteric artery
la arteria mesentérica superior	superior mesenteric artery
la arteria renal	renal artery
el cáliz renal	calyx
la capa cortical	cortex
la glándula suprarenal	suprarenal gland
el hilio renal	renal hilus
la medulla	medulla
la papila renal	renal papilla
la pelvis renal	renal pelvis
el riñón derecho	right kidney
el riñón izquierdo	left kidney
el tronco celiac	celiac trunk
el uréter	ureter
la uretra	urethra
la vejiga	urinary bladder
la vena cava inferior	inferior vena cava
la vena ilíaca común	common ilial vein
la vena renal	renal vein

El Sistema Digestivo (Digestive System)

el ano	anus
el apéndice	vermiform appendix
la cavidad bucal	oral cavity

el ciego	cecum
el colon ascendente	ascending colon
el colon descendente	descending colon
el colon sigmoideo	sigmoid colon
el colon transverse	transverse colon
el duodeno	duodenum
el esfínter anal	sphincter muscle of anus
el esófago	esophagus
el estómago	stomach
la faringe	pharynx
las glándulas salivales	salivary glands
el hígado	liver
el íleon	ileum
el intestino delgado	small intestine
el intestino grueso	large intestine
la lengua	Tongue
el pancreas	pancreas
el recto	rectum
la vesícula biliar	gallbladder
el yeyuno	jejunum

El Esqueleto (Skeleton)

Anterior	Anterior
el carpo	carpus
la clavícula	clavicle
el cóccix	coccyx
la columna vertebral	vertebral column
el cúbito	ulna
la doceava costilla	floating rib
el esternón	sternum
la falange	proximal phalanx
la falangeta	distal phalanx

la falangina	middle phalanx
el fémur	femur
la fíbula	fibula
el frontal	frontal bone
el hueso ilíaco	ilium
el hueso pómulo	zygomatic bone
el húmero	humerus
el maxilar inferior	mandible
el maxilar superior	maxilla
el metacarpo	metacarpus
el metatarso	metatarsus
el omóplato	scapula
la rótula	patella
el sacro	sacrum
el tarso	tarsus
el temporal	temporal bone
la tibia	tibia

Posterior	Posterior
el acromión	acromion
el astrágalo	talus
el atlas	atlas
el axis	axis
la cabeza del fémur	head of femur
la cabeza del húmero	head of humerus
el calcáneo	calcaneus
el cóndilo externo	lateral condyle of femur
el cóndilo interno	medial condyle of femur
la costilla falsa	false rib
el cuello del fémur	neck of femur
el epicóndilo	epicondyle
la epitroclea	epitrochlea
la espina del omóplato	spine of scapula

la falange	proximal phalanx
la falangeta	distal phalanx
la falangina	middle phalanx
el isquión	ischium
el occipital	occipital bone
el olécrano	olecranon
el omóplato	scapula
el parietal	parietal bone
el sacro	sacrum
el trocánter mayor	greater trochanter
las vértebras cervicales	cervical vertebra
las vértebras lumbares	lumbar vertebra
las vértebras lumbares	thoracic vertebra

El Sistema Nervioso Central (Central Nervous System)

el bulbo raquídeo	medulla oblongata
el cerebelo	cerebellum
el cerebro	cerebrum
la columna vertebral	vertibral column
el cuerpo calloso	corpus callosum
el cuerpo del fornix	body of fornix
la duramadre	dura mater
el fílum terminal	terminal filament
el filum terminal interno	internal filum terminale
la glándula pineal	pineal body
la hipófisis	pituitary gland
la médula espinal	spinal cord
la neurona sensorial	sensory neuron
la placa motriz	motor end plate
el puente de Varolio	pons Varolii
la quiasma óptico	optic chiasm
el receptor sensorial	sense receptor

| el septum lucidum | septum pellucidum |

El Sistema Nervioso Periférico (Peripheral Nervous System)

el nervio abdominogenital mayor	iliohypogastric nerve
el nervio abdominogenital menor	ilioinguinal nerve
el nervio ciático mayor	sciatic nerve
el nervio ciático menor	posterior thigh cutaneous nerve
el nervio ciático poplíteo externo	common peroneal nerve
el nervio ciático poplíteo interno	tibial nerve
el nervio circunflejo	axillary nerve
el nervio crural	femoral nerve
el nervio cubital	ulnar nerve
el nervio digital	digital nerve
el nervio femorocutánco	lateral thight cutaneous nerve
el nervio glúteo	gluteal nerve
el nervio intercostals	intercostal nerve
el nervio mediano	median nerve
el nervio obturador	obturator nerve
el nervio radial	radial nerve
el nervio safeno externo	sural nerve
el nervio safeno interno	saphenous nerve
el nervio tibial anterior	deep peroneal nerve
los nervios craneales	cranial nerves
el plexo braquial	brachial plexus
el plexo lumbar	lumbar plexus
el plexo sacro	sacral plexus

La Circulación de la Sangre (Blood Circulation)

la aorta abdominal	abdominal aorta
la arcada arterial	arch of foot artery
la arteria braquial	axillary artery

la arteria braquial	brachial artery
la arteria carótida primitive	common carotid artery
la arteria del dorso del pie	dorsalis pedis artery
la arteria femoral	femoral artery
la arteria ilíaca común	common iliac artery
la arteria ilíaca interna	internal iliac artery
la arteria mesentérica superior	superior mesenteric artery
la arteria pulmonary	pulmonary artery
la arteria renal	renal artery
la arteria subclavia	subclavian artery
la arteria tibial anterior	anterior tibial artery
el cayado de la aorta	arch of aorta
la vena axilar	axillary vein
la vena basilica	basilic vein
la vena cava inferior	inferior vena cava
la vena cava superior	superior vena cava
la vena cefálica	cephalic vein
la vena femoral	femoral vein
la vena mesentérica superior	superior mesenteric vein
la vena porta	portal vein
la vena pulmonary	pulmonary vein
la vena renal	renal vein
la vena safena interna	great saphenous vein
la vena subclavia	subclavian vein
la vena yugular externa	external jugular vein
la vena yugular interna	internal jugular vein

La Oreja (The Ear)

el canal	ear canal
el conducto auditivo	ear canal
el nervio auditivo	auditory nerve
el oido interno	inner ear

el oido medio	middle ear
la oreja	outer ear
el timpani	ear drum

El Ojo (The Eye)

la ceja	eyebrow
el conducto lagrimar	tear duct
la cornea	cornea
la esclerótica	sclera
el iris	iris
la lente	lens
el nervio óptico	optic nerve
el párpado	eyelid
el párpado inferior	lowcr cyclid
el párpado superior	upper eyelid
las pestañas	eyelashes
la pupila	pupil
la retina	retina

El Pie (The Foot)

la bola	ball
el dedo del pie	toe
el dedo gordo del pie	big toe
el empeine	instep
el pequeño dedo del pie	little toe
el talon	heel
el tobillo	ankle
la uña del dedo del pie	toenail
la yema	ball

La Mano (The Hand)

el dedo anular	ring finger
el dedo de enmedio	middle finger
el dedo índice	index finger
el dedo meñique	little finger
el dedo pulgar	thumb
la luñula	lunula
la muñeca	wrist
el nudillo	knuckle
la palma	Palm
la uña	Fingernail

El Corazón (The Heart)

la aorta	aorta
la arteria pulmonary	pulmonary trunk
la aurícula derecha	right atrium
la aurícula izquierda	left atrium
el cayado de la aorta	arch of aorta
el músculo papilar	papillary muscle
el tabique interventricular	interventricular septum
la válvula aortic	aortic valve
la válvula mitral	mitral valve
la válvula pulmonary	pulmonary valve
la válvula tricúspide	tricuspid valve
la vena cava inferior	inferior vena cava
la vena cava superior	superior vena cava
la vena pulmonar derecha	right pulmonary vein
la vena pulmonar izquierda	left pulmonary vein
el ventrículo derecho	left ventricle
el ventrículo derecho	right ventricle

Las Articulaciones (Joints)

la cadera	hip
el codo	elbow
el cuello	Neck
la espalda	Back
la espina dorsal	spine
el hombre	shoulder
la muñeca	Wrist
el nudillo	knuckle
la rodilla	Knee
el tobillo	ankle
la vertebra	vertebrae

Los Musculos (Muscles)

Anterior	Anterior
el aductor del muslo	long adductor
el bíceps braquial	arm biceps
el braquial anterior	brachial
el cubital anterior	the wrist's ulnar flexor
los deltoids	deltoids
el esternocleidomastoideo	sternocleidomastoid
el extensor común de los dedos del pie	long extensor of toes
el frontal	frontal
los gemelos	gastrocnemius
el interóseos del pie	plantar interosseous
el masetero	masseter
el oblicuo mayor	external oblique
el orbicular	orbicular of eye

el palmar mayor	flexor carpi radialis
el palmar menor	palmaris brevis
el pectoral mayor	greater pectoral
el pedio	short extensor of toes
el peroneo lateral largo	long peroneal
el pronador Redondo	round pronator
el recto anterior	straight muscle of thigh
el recto del abdomen	abdominal rectus
el sartorio	sartorius
el sóleo	soleus
el supinador largo	brachioradialis
el tensor de la fascia lata	tensor fascia lata
el tibial anterior	anterior tibial
el trapecio	trapezius
el vasto externo	medial great
el vasto interno	lateral great

Posterior	Posterior
el aductor mayor	great adductor
el ancóneo	anconeus
el bíceps crural	thigh biceps
el complexo mayor	complexus
el cubital anterior	flexor carpi ulnaris
el cubital posterior	extensor carpi ulnaris
el dorsal ancho	latissimus dorsi
el esplenio	splenius capitis muscles
el extensor común de los dedos	fingers' common extensor
los gemelos	gastrocnemius
el glúteo mayor	greatest gluteal
el infraspinoso	infraspinous
el oblicuo mayor del abdomen	external oblique
el occipital	occipital

el peroneo lateral corto	short peroneal
el plantar delgado	plantar
el radial externo primero	radial extensor wrist muscle - long
el radial externo Segundo	radial extensor wrist muscle - short
el recto interno del muslo	gracilis
el redondo mayor	teres major
el redondo menor	teres minor
el semimembranoso	semimembranous
el semitendinoso	semitendinous
el supinador largo	brachioradialis
el trapecio	trapezius
el tríceps braquial	brachial triceps
el vasto interno	lateral great

El Impulso sensorial (Sensory Impulse)

el axon	axon
los cuerpos de Nissl	axon hillock
la dendrite	dendrite
el ganglio espinal	spinal ganglion
la materia gris	gray matter
la neurona motriz	motor neuron
la neurona sensorial	sensory neuron
el nódulo de Ranvier	node of Ranvier
la placa motriz	motor end plate
la protoneurona	protoneuron
la raíz motriz	motor root
la raíz sensorial	sensory root
el receptor sensorial	sense receptor
la sinápsis	synapse
la substancia blanca	white matter
la vaina de mielina	myelin sheath

Las Células Animales (Animal Cells)

el aparato de Golgi	Golgi apparatus
el centriolo	centriole
la cromatina	chromatin
la lisosoma	lysosome
la membrana celulósica	cell membrane
la membrana nuclear	nuclear envelope
el mitocondrio	mitochondrion
el núcleo	nucleus
el nucléolo	nucleolus
el retículo endoplasmático	endoplasmic reticulum
la ribosoma	ribosome
la vacuole	vacuole
la vesícula pinocítica	pinocytotic vesicle

Chapter 3   - Common Medical History Questions

¿Cual es su nombre?	What is your name?
¿Cuantos años tiene usted?	How old are you?
¿Esta embarazada?	Are you pregnant?
¿Ha tenido alguna cirugía/operación?	Have you had any surgery?
¿Alguna hospitalización?	Other hospital confinement?
¿Alguna enfermedad grave?	Other serious illness?
¿Alguna herida grave?	Other serious injuries?
¿Tiene alergias?	Do you have allergies?
¿Usted fuma?	Do you smoke?
¿Usted bebe alcohol?	Do you drink alcohol?
¿Cuánto?	How much?
¿Desde hace cuánto?	How long?
¿Tienes calentura?	Do you have a fever?
¿Ha tenido cambios en la voz?	Have you had voice changes?
¿Donde te duele?	Where does it hurt?

Chapter 4 - Common Illnesses and Symptoms

Illnesses

acidez	heartburn
acné	acne
adicciones	addictions
alergias	allergies
anemia	anemia
anorexia	anorexia
ansiedad	anxiety
bronquitis	bronchitis
cancer	cancer
cataratas	cataracts
cólico	colic
conjuntivitis	pink eye
convulsiones	seizures
coresterol	cholesterol
cortes	cuts
depreción	depression
esmayo	fainting
iabetes	diabetes
diarrea	diarrhea
dolor	pain
dolor de garganta	sore throat
dolores	aches
dolores de cabeza	headaches
enfemedades venéreas	venereal disease
erupción	rash
esguinces	sprains
espasmos	spasms
estremecimiento	quiver
fiebre	fever
gripe	flu
hemorroides	hemorrhoids
hernia	hernia
hernia discal	slipped disc
hiperactividad	hyperactivity
hiperventilación	hyperventilation
impotencia	impotence
indigestión	indigestion
infecciones	infections
infecciones urinarias	urinary infections
insomnio	insomnia
mareo	dizziness

menopausia	menopause
migraña	migraine
morderse las uñas	nail biting
náuseas	nausea
nerviosismo	nervousness
neumonia	pneumonia
parálisis cerebral	cerebral palsy
picaduras	bites
presion alta	high blood pressure
problemas cardiacos	heart problems
problemas de espalda	back problems
problemas estomacales	stomach problems
problemas respiratorios	breathing problems
resfriados	colds
reumatismo	rheumatism
ronquidos	snoring
sangrado de nariz	nose bleeds
sarpullido	rash
senilidad	senility
sobrepeso	overweight
sordera	deafness
tartamudeo	stuttering
tos	coughs
tumores	tumors
ulceras	ulcers
varices	varicose veins
verrugas	warts
vertigo	dizziness
vómito	vomiting
xenofobia	xenophobia

Symptoms

la amigdalitis	tonsilitis
cansado/a	tired
la diarrea	diarrhea
el dolor de garganta	sore throat
el dolor pungent	throbbing pain
débil	weak
dolorido	sore
ensangrentado/a	bloody
el estornudo	sneeze
la fatiga	fatigue
la fiebre calenture	fever
hinchado/a	swollen

27

la hinchazón	swelling
la infección	infection
el moretón	bruise
la nariz mucosa	runny nose
la nausea	nausea
la sangria	bleeding
la tos	cough
el vertigo	dizziness

Common Complaints

Me mareo.	I feel dizzy.
Estoy con dolor.	I am in pain.
Estoy enfermo/enferma.	I'm sick.
Tengo diarrea.	I have diarrhea.
Tengo dolor de muelas.	I have a toothache.
Tengo frío.	I feel cold.
Tengo migraña.	I have a migraine.
Tengo vertigos.	I feel dizzy.

Los Signos Vitales (Vital Signs)

la bascule	scale
los latidos cardíacos irregulars	irregular heartbeat
el peso	weight
la presión	blood pressure
la presión alta	high blood pressure
la presión baja	low blood pressure
el pulso	pulse
el pulso lento	slow pulse
el pulso rápido	rapid pulse
la temperature	temperature

Talking about Pain

El dolor	The pain
¿Dónde le duele?	Where does it hurt?
¿Cómo es el dolor?	How is the pain?
¿Te duele la rodilla?	Did you hurt your knee?

Quality of Pain

agudo (m) /aguda (f)	sharp
punzante	sharp
punzante como un cuchillo	stabbing pain
pulsativo (m) pulsativa (f)	throbbing/pulsating
el dolor punzante	shooting pain
el dolor aplastante	crushing pain
doloroso (m), dolorasa (f)	aching
quemante	burning
de hormigueo	tingling
profundo (m), profunda (f)	deep
sordo (m), sorda (f)	dull
fijo (m), fija (f)	dull
molesto (m), molesta (f)	dull
la presión	pressure
la tension	tightness

Quantity of Pain

un poco	a little bit
regular, más o menos	medium
mucho (m), mucha (f)	a lot
fuerte	strong
moderado (m), moderada (f)	mild

Frequency of Pain

constante	constant
siempre	always
crónico (m), crónica (f)	chronic
intermitente	intermittent
todo el tiempo	all the time
va y viene	it comes and goes

Location of Pain

el dolor abdominal	abdominal pain
el dolor al lado	side pain
el dolor cuando orina	urinary pain
el dolor de cabeza	headache
el dolor de cadera	hip pain
el dolor de codo	elbow pain

el dolor de espalda	back pain
el dolor de garganta	sore throat
el dolor de las articulaciones	joint pain
el dolor de los músculos	muscle pain
el dolor de mano	hand pain
el dolor de muñeca	wrist pain
el dolor de pantorrilla	calf pain
el dolor de pie	foot pain
el dolor de pierna	leg pain
el dolor de rodilla	knee pain
el dolor de tobillo	ankle pain
el dolor del cuello	neck pain
el dolor del estómago	stomach pain
el dolor del hombre	shoulder pain
el dolor del oído	earache
el dolor en el escroto	scrotal pain
el dolor en el pecho	chest pain
el dolor en la matriz	uterine pain
el dolor en los dientes	dental pain
el dolor en los ovaries	ovarian pain
el dolor menstrual	menstrual pain

Chapter 5 - Medicines and Treatments

Los Medicamentos y Los Tratamientos

la amputación	amputation
los analgésicos	analgesics
el análisis	analysis
los antiácidos	antacids
los antibióticos	antibiotics
el antidepresivo	antidepressant
el antidote	antidote
el antigripal	cold relief medicine
los antihistamínicos	antihistamines
el antiseptic	antiseptic
el antitetánico	antitetanic
la aspirina	aspirin
el atomizador	spray
la venda	bandage
el bicarbonate	bicarbonate
la cápsula	capsule
la circuncisión	circumcision
la codeina	codeine
la cortisona	cortisone
la crema para comezón	anti-itching cream
el descongestionante	decongestant
el diurético	diuretic
el elixir	elixir
el esteroide	steriod
el estrógeno	estrogen
el expectorante	expectorant
el ácido fólico	folic acid
las gotas	drops
las gotas para los ojos	eye drops
la gragea	coated pill
la hipnosis	hypnosis
la histerectomía	hysterectomy
las hormonas	hormones
el inhalador	inhaler
la insulin	insulin
la inyección	injection
el jarabe	syrup
el jarabe para la tos	cough syrup
la laparoscopía	laparoscopy
el laxante	laxative
el liniment	liniment

el liquid	liquid
la loción	lotion
el medicamento	medication
la medicina	medicine
la obturación	dental filling
el parche	patch
la pastille	lozenge
la pastille	pill
la penicilina	penicillin
la píldora	pill
el polvo	powder
la pomade	cream
la potencia	potency
el purgante	purgative
la quimioterapia	chemotherapy
el sedante	sedative
el supositorio	suppository
la suspension	suspension
la tablet	tablet
el tónico	tonic
los tranquilizantes	tranquilizers
la transfusión de sangre/sanguínea	blood transfusion
el ungüento	ointment
la vitamina	vitamin
el yeso	plaster cast

Instructions for Taking Medicine

Tome esta medicina...	Take this medicin...
____ veces al día.	____ times a day.
cada ____ horas	every __ hours
disuelta en agua	dissolved in water
con cada comida	with each meal
antes de cada comida	before each meal
después de cada comida	after each meal
antes de acostarse	before going to bed

Disuelva una tablet/pastilla debajo de la lengua.
Dissolve a tablet under your tongue.

Este medicamento puede causar sueño/somnolencia.
This medication may cuase drowsiness.

Agite bien antes de usar.
Shake well before using.

Manténgala refrigerada.
Keep it refrigerated.

General Instructions

Doble las rodillas.	Bend your knees.
Estire sus brazos.	Extend your arms.
Abra la boca.	Open your mouth.
Saque la lengua.	Stick your tongue out.
Respire rápido.	Breathe quickly.
Respire despacio/lento.	Breath slowly.
Aquarante la respiración.	Hold your breath.
Respire profundo.	Take a deep breath.
Venga en ayunas.	Come with an empty stomach.
Acuéstese sobre la mesa.	Lie down on the table.
Póngase boca arriba.	Turn face up.
Póngase boca abajo.	Turn face down.
Trague saliva.	Swallow saliva.
Silbe, por favor.	Whistle, please.
Sonría, por favor.	Smile, please.
Diga aaah.	Say aaah.
Regresa a ver me en una semana.	Come back and see me in one week.

Chapter 6 - Newborn

Common Terms:

recién nacido/a	newborn
el bebé	baby, baby boy
la bebé	baby girl
el bebé prematuro	premature baby
la cesárea	cesarean section
el pediatra	pediatrician
dar el pecho	to breastfeed
la lactancia materna	breast feeding
la leche de fórmula	formula milk
la lactancia artificial	bottle feeding
la lactancia mixta	a mix of breast and bottle feeding
el biberón	bottle
el chupete	pacifier
a tetina	teat
el babero	bib
la cuna	crib, cot
la cuna mecedora	cradle
el juguete	toy
el cochecito de bebé	baby carriage
el pañal	diaper
el cambiador	changer
el orinal	potty
la papilla	pureed baby food
la leche	milk
llorar	to cry
reir	to laugh
esterilizar	to sterilize
el esterilizador	sterilizer
e calienta biberones	bottle warmer
el desarrollo	development
la dermatitis del pañal	diaper rash
la crema para irritaciones	nappy cream
el cólico	colic

Chapter 7 - Nutrition

General Terms

la nutrición	nutrition
la desnutrición	malnutrition
la estatura	height
el peso	weight
gráfica te peso	weight chart

Measuring Units and utensils

la libra	pound	
el cuarto		quart
cuarto/a		quarter
la docena		dozen
el galón	gallon	
el kilogramo		kilogram
el gramo		gram
el miligramo		milligram
el gramo		gram
el litro		liter
el mililitro		milliliter
la onza	ounce	
centígrado/a		centigrade
fahrenheit		fahrenheit
la taza		cup
la taza para medir		measuring cup
la cuchara de medir		measuring spoon
el tenedor		fork
el vaso		glass
el cuchillo		knife
el plato	plate	
el platillo		saucer

Meals

la comida	food
el menú	menu
el desayuno	breakfast

el almuerzo	lunch
la cena	dinner
el ayuno	fast
el apetito	appetite
el sabor	flavor
la dieta	diet
la digestión	digestion
el plato	dish, plate
la bebida	drink
la rehidratación	rehydration

Taste

amargo/amarga	bitter
picante	spicy
grasoso/grasosa	fatty, greasy
salado/salada	salty
agrio/agria	sour
dulce	sweet
sabroso/sabrosa	tasty
sin sabor	tasteless
pequeño/ pequeñoa	size
sólido/sólida	solid

Food preparation

asado/asada	baked, broiled
hervido/hervida	boiled
empanado/empanada	breaded
dorado/dorada	browned
picado/picada	chopped
cocido/cocida	cooked
cortado/cortada en cubitos	diced
seco/seca	dried
frito/frita	fried
fresco/fresco	fresh
machacado/machacada	mashed
ahumado/ahumada	smoked
tostado/tostada	toasted
cocido/cocida a vapor	steam
tierno/tierna	tender
podrido/podrida	rotten
el puré	puree
puro/pura	pure
mojado/mojada	wet

batido/batida   whipped

Nutrients

la proteína	protein
la proteína completa	complete protein
la proteína complementaria	complementary protein
la cafeína	caffeine
el calcio	calcium
la caloría	calorie
el carbohidrato	carbohydrate
la glucosa	glucose
el colesterol	cholesterol
el yodo	iodine
el hierro	iron
los minerales	los minerals
la vitamina	vitamins

Chapter 8 - Medical Tests

la ecografía	ultrasound
la prueba del embarazo	pregnancy test
el rayo X	X-ray
el análisis de orina	urine test
la fecalysis	fecalysis
la mamografía	the mammogram
la resonancia magnética	magnetic resonance imaging (MRI)
la coronariografía	coronary angiogram
la endoscopia	endoscopy
la colonoscopía	colonoscopy
la biopsia	biopsy
la electrocardiografía	electrocardiography (ECG)
la electroencefalografía	electroencephalography (EEG)

Spanish-English Medical Dictionary

A

abdomen (m)	abdomen
abdominal (adj)	abdominal
ablandador fecal (m)	stool softener
aborto (m)	abortion
aborto inducido (m)	induced abortion
aborto involuntario (m)	miscarriage
aborto natural (m)	miscarriage
aborto terapéutico (m)	therapeutic abortion
abrasión (f)	abrasion
absceso (m)	abscess
absceso perianal (m)	perianal abscess
absorción (f)	absorption
abstinencia (f)	abstinance
abuso (m)	abuse
ácaro (m)	mite
ácaros del polvo (m/pl)	dust mite
accidente (m)	accident

acetaminofén (m)	acetaminophen
acidez estomacal (f)	heartburn
ácido (adj)	acid
ácido fólico (m)	folic acid
ácido úrico (m)	uric acid
acné (f)	acne
aconsejar (vb)	to advise
activo (adj)	active
acupuntura (f)	acupuncture
adhesion (f)	adhesion
adicción (f)	addiction
adicción a las drogas (f)	drug addiction
adicto (m), adicta (f)	addict
adolescencia (f)	adolescence
adolescente (m/f)	adolescent, teenager
adolorido (adj)	tender
adopción (f)	adoption
adoptar (vb)	to adopt
adoptivo/adoptiva (adj)	adopted
adormecimiento (m)	numbness
adrenalina (f)	adrenaline
adulto (m), adulta (f)	adult
afeitar(se) (vb)	to shave
afligirse (vb)	to grieve
agente (m/f)	agent
agitación (f)	agitation
agotamiento (m)	exhaustion
agrandamiento (m)	enlargement
agua (m)	water
agudo (adj)	acute, sharp (pain)
aguijón (m)	sting
aguja (f)	needle
ahogamiento (m)	drowning
ahogar(se) (vb)	to choke, to drown
aire (m)	air
aislar (vb)	isolate
alarcrán (m)	scorpion
albacora (f)	albacore
albino (m), albina (f)	albino
albúmina (f)	albumin
alcalosis (f)	alkalosis
alcohólico (m), alcohólica (f)	alcoholic
alcoholismo (m)	alcoholism
alérgeno (m)	allergen
alergia (f)	allergy
alergia a los alimentos (f)	food allergy

alérgico (adj)	allergic
alergista (m/f)	allergist
alerta (adj)	alert
aliento (m)	breath
alimentación (f)	food, nourishment
alimentación equilibrada (f)	balanced diet
alimentar (vb)	to feed
alimentos (m/pl)	food, nourishment
alimentos picantes (m/pl)	spicy foods
alivio (m)	relief
almohada (f)	pillow
almohadilla eléctrica (f)	heating pad
alopecia (f)	alopecia
altura (f)	height
alvéolos (m/pl)	alveoli
alucinación (f)	halucination
amargo/amarga (adj)	bitter
ambidextro (adj)	ambidextrous
ambulancia (f)	ambulance
amenorrea (f)	amenorrhea
amígdala (f)	tonsil
amigdalectomía (f)	tonsillectomy
amigdalitis (f)	tonsillitis
aminoácido (m)	amino acid
amnesia (f)	amnesia
amniocentesis (f)	amniocentesis
amoníaco (m)	ammonia
amoratado/amoratada (adj)	bruised
ampolla (f)	blister
ampolla de fiebre (f)	fever blister
amputación (f)	amputation
amputado (m), amputada (f)	amputee
amputar (vb)	to amputate
analgesia epidural (f)	epidural analgesia
analgésico (m)	analgesic, pain reliever
análisis (m)	analysis
análisis de orina (m)	urinalysis
anatomía (f)	anatomy
anciano (adj)	elderly
andador (m)	walker
andropausia-climaterio masculine (f)	andropause
anemia (f)	anemia
anemia de células falciformes (f)	sickle cell anemia
anémico (adj)	anemic
anestesia (f)	anesthesia
anestesia intravenosa(f)	intravenous anesthesia
anestesiólogo (m), anestesióloga (f)	anesthesiologist

aneurisma (m)	aneurysm, aneurism
anfetaminas (f/pl)	amphetamines
angina de pecho (f)	angina, chest pain
angiograma (m)	angiogram
angioplastia (f)	angioplasty
angustiado/angustiada (adj)	distressed
ano (m)	anus
anorexia (f)	anorexia
anormal (adj)	abnormal
anormalidad (f)	abnormality
anquilostomosis (f)	hookworm
ansiedad (f)	anxiety
ansioso/ansiosa (adj)	anxious
antebrazo (m)	forearm
antepasado (m), antepasada (f)	ancestor
antiácido (m)	antacid
antibacteriano (f)	antibacterial
antibiótico (m)	antibiotic
anticoagulante (m)	anticoagulant
anticoncepción (f)	contraception
anticonceptivo (m)	contraceptive
anticuerpos (m/pl)	antibodies
antidepresivo (m)	antidepressant
antídoto (m)	antidote
anti-inflamatorio (m)	anti-inflammatory
antihistamínico (m)	antihistamine
antipalúdico (m)	antimalarial
antiseptico (m)	antiseptic
antojo (m)	craving
ántrax (m)	anthrax
anualmente (adj)	yearly
aorta (f)	aorta
aparato ortopédico (m)	brace
apatía (f)	apathy
apendectomía (f)	appendectomy
apéndice (m)	appendix
apendicitis (f)	appendicitis
apendis (m)	appendicitis
apetito (m)	appetite
aplicador (m)	applicator, swab
apnea (f)	apnea
apnea del sueño (f)	sleep apnea
ardor de estomago	heartburn
arrastrar las palabras (vb)	to slur
arritmia (f)	arrhythmia
arrojar (vb)	to throw up

arrojos (m/pl)	vomit
arteria (f)	artery
articulaciones (f/pl)	joints
artritis (f)	arthritis
artritis reumatoide (f)	rheumatoid arthritis
asbesto (m)	asbestos
aseo (m)	hygiene
asfixia (f)	asphyxia
asistencia (f)	help
asistente médico profesional (m/f)	physician's assistant
asma (m)	asthma
asma bronquial (m)	bronchial asthma
asmático/asmática (adj)	asthmatic
aspirina (f)	aspirin
astigmatismo (m)	astigmatism
astilla (f)	sliver, splinter
ataque (m)	heart attack
ataque cardíaco (m)	heart attack
ataque de calor (m)	heat stroke
ataque de pánico (m)	panic attack
atención médica (f)	health care
atrio (m)	atrium
atrofia (f)	atrophy
atrofiarse (vb)	to atrophy
aturdido/aturdida (adj)	dazed
aturdimiento (m)	daze
audición (f)	hearing
audífonos (m/pl)	hearing aids
autismo (m)	autism
autoexámen de mama (m)	breast self-examination
autopsia (f)	autopsy
aviso (m)	warning
axila (f)	arm pit
ayuda (f)	help
ayudante de enfermero (m/f)	nurse's aide
ayudar (vb)	to help
ayunar (vb)	to fast

B

babero (m)	bib
bacteria (f)	bacteria
baja en calorias (adj)	low calorie
balanza (f)	scale
balazo (m)	bullet
bañar(se) (vb)	to bathe

baño (m)	bath
baños de asiento (m/pl)	sitz-baths
barbilla (f)	chin
barbitúricos (m/pl)	barbiturates
bario (m)	barium
bastón (m)	cane
bata (f)	gown
bazo (m)	spleen
bebé (m)	baby
beber (vb)	to drink
bebida (f)	beverage
beneficios (m/pl)	benefits
benigno (adj)	benign
beso (m)	kiss
bíceps (m)	biceps
bicúspide (m)	bicuspid
bienestar (asistencia social) (f)	welfare
bifocales (m/pl)	bifocals
bilirrubina (f)	bilirubin
bilis (f)	bile
biológico (adj)	biological
biopsia (f)	biopsy
bizco/bizca (adj)	cross-eyed
blefaritism (f)	blepharitis
boca (f)	mouth
boca abajo	face down
boca arriba	face up
boca seca (f)	dry mouth
bocio (m)	goiter
bolsa amniótica (f)	amniotic sac
bomba (f)	pump
bombero (m), bombera(f)	firefighter
borracho/borracha (adj)	drunk
bostezar (vb)	to yawn
bostezo (m)	yawn
botella (f)	bottle
botulismo (m)	botulism
brazo (m)	arm
bronquio (m)	bronchus
bronquitis (f)	bronchitis
bulimia (f)	bulimia
bulímico/bulímica (adj)	bulimic
bulto (m)	lump
bursitis (f)	bursitis

cabello (m, col)	hair (of head)
cabestrillo (m)	sling
cabeza (f)	head, temple
cachete (m, col)	cheek
cada día (adv)	daily
cadera (f)	hip
caer(se) (vb)	to fall
cafeína (f)	caffeine
caída (f)	fall
caída de la mollera (f, col)	fallen/sunken fontanelle
caída del recto (f)	rectal prolapse
caída rápida (f)	collapse
caja de cultivo (f)	Petri dish
caja de Petri (f)	Petri dish
caja toráxica (f)	rib cage
calambres (m/pl)	cramps
calambres en las piernas (m/pl)	leg cramps
calambres musculares (m/pl)	muscular cramps
calambres uterinos (m/pl)	uterine cramps
calavera (f, col)	skull
calcificado/calcificada (adj)	calcified
calcio (m)	calcium
cálculos (m/pl)	kidney stones
cálculos biliares (m/pl)	gallstones
cálculos en el riñón (m/pl)	kidney stones
cálculos en la vejiga (m/pl)	bladder stones
cálculos en la vesícula (m/pl)	gallstones
calentura (f, col)	fever
callado/callada (adj)	quiet
callo (m)	callous, corn
calmante (m)	sedative, analgesic, tranquilizer
calmante para el dolor (m)	pain reliever
calores (m/pl, col)	hot flashes
caloría (f)	calorie
calosfríos (m/pl)	hot flashes
calostro (m)	colostrum
calvicie (f)	baldness
calvo (m), calva(f)	bald
cama (f)	bed
cambio de humor (m)	mood swing
cambio de peso (m)	weight change
cambio de vida (m, col)	menopause
cambios visuales (m/pl)	visual changes

camilla (f)	gurney, stretcher
caminar (vb)	to walk
caminar dormido (vb)	to sleepwalk
camisa de fuerza (f)	straight jacket
camita (f)	crib
canal (m)	ear canal
canal del parto (m)	birth canal
canal en la raíz (m)	root canal
cáncer (m)	cancer
cáncer de piel (m)	skin cancer
canceroso/cancerosa (adj)	cancerous
cangrena (f, col)	gangrene
canicas (f/pl, col)	brain
canino (m)	canine tooth, eyetooth
caño (m)	urethra
cañón (m)	urethra
cansado/cansada (adj)	tired, weary
cansancio (m)	tiredness, fatigue
capilar (m)	capillary
cápsula (f)	capsule
cara (f)	face
cara aceitosa (f)	oily face
cara grasosa (f)	oily face
carbohidrato (m)	carbohydrate
carcinogénico/carcinogénica (adj)	carcinogenic
carcinoma (m)	carcinoma
cardenal (m, col)	bruise
cardíaco/cardíaca (adj)	cardiac
cardialgia (f)	heartburn
cardiología (f)	cardiology
cardiólogo (m), cardióloga (f)	cardiologist
carencia (f)	deficiency
careta de oxígeno (f)	oxygen mask
cariado/cariada (adj)	decayed
caries (f)	dental cavities
carta para agudeza visual (f)	eye chart
cartílago (m)	cartilage
casco de la cabeza (m, col)	scalp
caspa (f)	dandruff
castración (f)	castration
catarata (f)	cataract
catarro (m)	congestion
catarro de pecho (m)	bronchitis, chest cold
catatónico/catatónica (adj)	catatonic
catéter (m)	catheter
cateterismo (m)	catheterization

cateterizar (vb)	to catheterize
causa (f)	cause
cauterizar (vb)	to cauterize
cavidad hueca (f)	sinus
ceceo (m)	lisp
cedrulla (m)	ear wax
cefalea (f)	headache
ceguera (f)	blindness
ceja (f)	eyebrow
células (f/pl)	cells
células blancas de sangre (f/pl)	white blood cells
células rojas de sangre (f/pl)	red blood cells
células sanguíneas (f/pl)	blood cells
centro infantil (m)	day-care center
cepillo de dientes (m)	toothbrush
cerebro (m)	brain, neck, fontanelle
cerilla (f)	ear wax
certificado de nacimiento (m)	birth certificate
cera del oído (f)	ear wax
cerumen (m)	ear wax
cérvix (f)	cervix
chamorro (m, col)	calf (of the leg)
chata (f)	bedpan
chequear (vb)	to examine
chequeo (m)	checkup
chichón (m)	bump
chillarle (vb)	to wheeze
chillido (m)	wheeze
chinaloa (f)	opium
chinche (f)	bedbug
choque (m)	shock, nervous breakdown
chorro (m, col)	gonorrhea
chucho (m)	cleft palate
chueco (m)	clubfoot
chupete (m)	pacifier, bottle nipple
chupón (m)	pacifier
cianosis (f)	cyanosis
ciática (f)	sciatica
ciático/ciática (adj)	sciatic
cicatriz (f)	scar
ciclo menstrual (m)	menstrual cycle
ciego/ciega (adj)	blind
ciego (m), ciega (f)	blind person
cieno (m)	ooze
cigarrillo (m)	cigarette
cintura (f)	lower back, waist

circulación (f)	circulation
circuncidar (vb)	to circumcise
circuncisión (f)	circumcision
cirrosis (f)	cirrhosis
cirrosis hepática (f)	cirrhosis
cirugía (f)	surgery
cirugía abdominal (f)	abdominal surgery
cirugía cosmética (f)	cosmetic surgery
cirugía dental (f)	dental surgery
cirugía electiva (f)	elective surgery
cirugía laser (f)	laser surgery
cirugía ortopédica (f)	orthopedic surgery
cirugía plástica (f)	face-lift, plastic surgery
cirujano (m), cirujana (f)	surgeon
cirujano bariátrico (m)	bariatric surgeon
cirujano ortopédico (m)	orthopedic surgeon
cirujana ortopédica (f)	orthopedic surgeon
cirujano plástico (m)	plastic surgeon
cirujana plástica (f)	plastic surgeon
cistitis (f)	cystitis
cita (f)	appointment
citología (f)	cytology
clamidia (f)	chlamydia
claustrofobia (f)	claustrophobia
clavícula (f)	collarbone
cleptomanía (f)	kleptomania
clínica (f)	clinic
clítoris (f)	clitoris
coágulo (m)	clot
coágulo de sangre (m)	blood clot
cocaína (f)	cocaine
cóccix, cocciz (m)	coccyx, tailbone
cochecillo (m)	stroller
codeína (f)	codeine
codo (m)	elbow
codo de golfista (m)	golfer's elbow
codo de tenista (m)	tennis elbow
cogote (m, col)	Adam's apple
coito (m)	coitus
cojear (vb)	to limp
cojera (f)	limp
cojín eléctrico (m)	heating pad
cojo/coja (adj)	lame, crippled
cojo (m), coja (f)	crippled person
colágeno (m)	collagen
colapso (m)	collapse, shock

colapso mental (m)	nervous breakdown
colapso nervioso (m)	nervous breakdown
colar (vb)	to strain
colecistitis (f)	cholecystitis
cólera (m)	cholera
colesterol (m)	cholesterol
colesterol alto (m)	high cholesterol
cólico (m)	colic
cólicos (m/pl, col)	abdominal cramps
cólicos menstruales (m/pl)	menstrual cramps
colita (f)	tailbone, coccyx
colitis (f)	colitis, diarrhea
collar (m)	neck brace
colon (m)	colon
colonoscopía (f)	colonoscopy
colorado/colorada (adj)	flushed
colostomia (f)	colostomy
colostro (m)	colostrum
columna (f, col)	backbone, spine
columna vertebral (f)	spine, spinal column
coma (f)	coma
comadrona (f)	midwife
comatoso/comatosa (adj)	comatose
combatir (vb)	to fight
comer (vb)	to eat
comezón (f)	itch, prickling
comida (f)	nourishment, food
comidita de bebé (f)	baby food
comido de la luna (m)	cleft palate
cómodo/cómoda (adj)	comfortable
compañía de seguro (f)	insurance company
complicación (f)	complication
componer (vb)	to get well
compresa (f)	compress
compresa caliente (f)	hot pack
compresión (f)	contusion
concebir (vb)	to conceive
concepción (f)	conception
conciencia (f)	consciousness
concusión de la espina cervical (f)	whiplash
condición (f)	condition
condón (m)	condom
conducta (f)	behavior
conducto (m)	tube
conducto auditivo (m)	auditory canal
conducto auditivo externo (m)	ear canal
conducto lacrimar (m)	tear duct

conducto lagrimar (m)	tear duct
conducto radicular(m)	root canal
confidencialidad (f)	confidentiality
confortable (adj)	comfortable
confundido/confundida (adj)	confused
confusión (f)	confusion
congelado (m)	frostbite
congelamiento (m)	frostbite
congelar (vb)	to freeze
congénito/congénita (adj)	congenital
congestión (f, col)	congestion
congestión nasal (f)	sinus congestion
congestionado/congestionada (adj)	congested
conjuntiva (f)	conjunctiva
conjuntivitis (f)	conjunctivitis, pinkeye
conmoción cerebral (f)	concussion
conocimiento (m)	consciousness
consciente (adj)	conscious
consejería (f)	counseling
consejero (m)/consejera (f)	counselor
consejo (m)	advice, recommendation
consentimiento (m)	consent
consentimiento informado (m)	informed consent
consentir (vb)	to consent
constipación (m)	constipation
constipado (m)	congestion
constipado/constipada (adj)	constipated
consulta (f)	consult
consultar (vb)	to consult
consultorio (m)	doctor's office
contagioso/contagiosa (adj)	contagious
contaminado/contaminada (adj)	contaminated
contracciones (f/pl)	contractions
contracepción (f)	contraception
contraceptivo (m)	contraceptive
contusión (f)	contusion, trauma
convalesciente (m/f)	convalescent
convulsión (f)	convulsion, siezure
convulsiones (m/pl)	seizures
coqueluche (m/f)	whooping cough,
pertussis	
corazón (m)	heart
cordal (m)	wisdom tooth
cordón umbilical (m)	umbilical cord
cordura (f)	sanity
corona (f)	crown (dental)

coronario/coronaria (adj)	coronary
coronilla (f)	crown
cortada (f)	cut
cortar (vb)	to cut
corte (m)	cut
cortina (f)	drape
cortisona (f)	cortisone
corto de vista (m, col)	myopia
cortocircuito (m)	shunt
coser (vb)	to stitch up
costado (m, col)	side (of the body)
costilla (f)	rib, rib cage
costra (f)	scab
costumbre (f)	habit
coyuntura (f, col)	joint
cráneo (m)	cranium, skull
crecimiento (m)	growth
creencia (f)	belief
crema (f)	cream
criar (vb)	to nurture
criatura (f)	baby, infant
criocirugía (f)	cryosurgery
crisis nerviosa (f)	nervous breakdown
crítico/crítica (adj)	critical
crónico/crónica (adj)	chronic
cruda (f)	hangover
crup (m)	croup
Cruz Roja (f)	Red Cross
cuádriceps (m)	quadriceps
cuadril (m, col)	hip, hipbone
cuadro (m)	chart
cuajo (m, col)	blood clot
cuajarón (m, col)	blood clot
cuarentena (f)	quarantine
cuate (m/f)	twin
cuarto de los niños (m)	nursery
cucharada (f)	tablespoon
cucharadita (f)	teaspoon
cuchillada (f)	gash
cuchillo (m)	knife
cuello (m)	neck
cuello de la matriz (m, col)	cervix
cuello rígido (m)	stiff neck
cuello uterino (m)	cervix
cuenta (f)	bill
cuerda vocal (f)	vocal cord
cuerdo/cuerda (adj)	sane

cuero (m, col)	facial skin
cuero cabelludo (m)	scalp
cuerpo (m)	body
cuerpo adolorido (m)	aching all over
cuerpo quebrado (m)	aching all over
cuidado (m)	care
cuidado intensivo neonatal (m)	neonatal intensive care
cuidado postnatal (m)	postnatal care
cuidado prenatal (m)	prenatal care
culebrilla (f)	shingles, ringworm
culpa (f)	guilt
cultivo de la garganta (m)	throat culture
cuna (f)	crib
cuota (f)	quota
curado/curada (adj)	cured
curanderismo (m)	folk healing
curandero (m), curandera (f)	folk healer
curar (vb)	to treat, cure
curarse (vb)	to heal, recover
curita (f)	bandaid
custodia (f)	custody
cutícula (f)	cuticle

D

daltonismo (m)	color-blindness
dañado/dañada (adj)	impaired
dañar (vb)	to harm
dañino/dañina (adj)	harmful
daño (m)	injury, lesion, damage
daño cerebral (m)	brain damage
dar (vb)	to give
dar a luz (vb)	to deliver a baby, to give birth to
dar al galillo (vb)	to choke
dar de alta (vb)	to discharge
dar de comer (vb)	to feed
dar el masaje (vb)	to massage, rub
dar el pecho (vb)	to breastfeed
dar medicina (vb)	to medicate
débil (adj)	weak, faint
debilidad (f)	weakness
debilidad de los músculos (f)	muscle weakness
decaido/decaida (adj)	weak
decaimiento (m, col)	fatigue

dedito (m, col)	little finger
dedo (m)	finger
dedo del pie (m)	toe
dedo gordo (m)	thumb
defecar (vb)	to defecate
defecto congénito (m)	congenital defect
defecto de nacimiento (m)	birth defect
defibrilador (m)	defibrillator
deficiencia (f)	deficiency
deformación (f)	deformity
deformado/deformada (adj)	deformed
deformidad (f)	deformity
defunción (f)	death
deglutir (vb)	to swallow
dejar de (vb)	to quit
delantal de plomo (m)	lead apron
delgado/delgada (adj)	thin
delirando/deliranda (adj)	delirious
delirante (adj)	delirious
delirio (m)	delusion, delirium
deltoides (m/pl)	deltoids
demacrado/demacrada (adj)	emaciated
demencia (f)	insanity, dementia
demente (adj)	insane
dentadura (f)	denture
dentadura postiza (f)	false teeth
dental (adj)	dental
dentario/dentaria (adj)	dental
dentición (f)	teething
dentista (m/f)	dentist
dependencia de las drogas (f)	drug addiction
deponer (vb)	to vomit, throw up
depresión (f)	depression
depresión posparto (f)	postpartum depression
depresor (m)	tongue depressor
depresor de lengua (m)	tongue depressor
deprimido/deprimada (adj)	depressed
derecha (f)	right
dermatitis (f)	dermatitis
dermatólogo (m), dermatóloga (f)	dermatologist
derrame cerebral (m)	stroke, cerebral hemorrhage
desahogo (m)	relief
desaldillado (m)	hernia
desangramiento (m)	bleeding
desarollar (vb)	to develop
desarollo (m)	development
descansar (vb)	to rest, relax

descanso en cama (m)	bed rest
descarga (f)	discharge
descongestionante (m)	decongestant
descongestivo (m)	decongestant
desconsolado/desconsolada (adj)	uncomfortable
descontinuar (vb)	to discontinue
descremado/descremada (adj)	fat-free
desecho (m)	breast/nasal/vaginal discharge/flow
deseo sexual (m)	libido, sexual desire
desesperado (adj)	hopeless, desperate
desfallecimientos (m/pl)	fainting spells
desfibrilación (f)	defibrillation
desfigurado/desfigurada (adj)	deformed
desfigurar (vb)	to disfigure
desgano (m)	lack of appetite
desgarramiento (m)	muscle or ligament tear
desgarro (m)	muscle or ligament tear
desgarro (m)	torn ligament
desgonzamiento (m, col)	weakness, nervous breakdown
desgonzarse (vb, col)	to be anxious
deshabilitado/deshabilitada (adj)	handicapped
deshecho (m)	discharge
deshidración (f)	dehydration
desinfectante (m)	disinfectant
desinfectar (vb)	to disinfect
desmayar(se) (vb)	to faint
desmayos (m/pl)	fainting spells
desnudo/desnuda (adj)	naked
desnutrición (f)	malnutrition
desorden (m)	disorder
desorden nervioso (m)	nervous disorder
desorientación (f)	disorientation
despachar (vb)	to fill in
despertar (vb)	to wake up, awaken
despertarse (vb)	to wake up
despierto/despierta (adj)	awake
despigmentación (f)	depigmentation
desprendimiento de la retina (m)	detached retina
después de la operación (adj)	post-op
destetar (vb)	to wean
desvanecer (vb, col)	to faint
desviación (f)	shunt
deterioro (m)	deterioration
detoxificación (f)	detoxification

devolver (vb)	to throw up
diabetes (f)	diabetes
diabetis (f, col)	diabetes
diabetes gestacional (f)	gestational diabetes
diabético/diabética (adj)	diabetic
diabetic (m), diabética (f)	diabetic person
diafragma (m)	diaphragm
diagnosticado/diagnosticada (adj)	diagnosed
diagnosticar (vb)	to diagnose
diagnóstico (m)	diagnosis
diálisis (f)	dialysis
diariamente (adv)	daily
diario/diaria (adj)	every day, daily
diarrea (f)	dysentery, diarrhea
dichoso/dichosa (adj)	happy
diente (m)	tooth
diente impactado (m)	impacted tooth
dientes podridos (m/pl)	dental cavities
dientes postizos (m/pl)	false teeth
dieta (f)	diet
dietista (m/f)	dietitian
difteria (f)	diphtheria
difunto/difunta (adj)	deceased
difunto (m), difunta (f)	dead person
digerir (vb)	to digest
digestión (f)	digestion
dilatación (f)	dilation
dilatación y curetaje (f)	dilatation & curettage – D&C
dilatado/dilatada (adj)	dilated
diluido/diluida (adj)	dilute
diluir (vb)	to dilute
diluyente de la sangre (m)	blood thinner
dipleja espástica (f)	cerebral palsy
dipsomanía (f)	alcoholism
discapacidad (f)	disability
discapacitado/discapacitada (adj)	handicapped
disco desplazado (m)	slipped disk
disentería (f)	dysentery
disfunción erectile (f)	erectile dysfunction
dislexia (f)	dyslexia
dislocación (f)	dislocation
dislocar (vb)	to sprain
dismenorrea (f)	dysmenorrhea
dispositivo intrauterino (DIU) (m)	intrauterine device - IUD
distender(se) (vb)	to distend
distensión abdominal (f)	abdominal distention
distrofia (f)	dystrophy

distrofia muscular (f)	muscular dystrophy
disuria (f)	dysuria
diurético (m)	diuretic
doctor (m), doctora (f)	physician, doctor
dolencia (f)	ailment, earache
doler (vb)	to hurt
dolor (m)	pain, ache
dolor adormecedor (m)	numbing pain
dolor agudo (m)	sharp pain
dolor aplastante (m)	crushing pain
dolor crónico (m)	chronic pain
dolor cuando orina (m)	urinary pain
dolor de aire (m)	ulcer, back pain
dolor de cabeza (m)	headache
dolor de cuello (m)	neck pain
dolor de dientes (m)	toothache
dolor de espalda (m)	back pain
dolor de garganta (m)	sore throat
dolor de las articulaciones (m)	joint pain
dolor de matriz (m)	uterine pain
dolor de muelas (m)	toothache
dolor de músculos (m)	muscle pain
dolor de oído (m)	earache
dolor de panza (m)	abdominal cramps
dolor de pecho (m)	chest pain
dolor de riñones (m)	back pain
dolor de útero (m)	uterine pain
dolor del costado (m)	flank pain
dolor del cuerpo (m)	body pain
dolor del estómago (m)	stomach ache, stomach pain
dolor durante la regla (m)	menstrual pain
dolor en los ovarios (m)	ovarian pain
dolor intermitente (m)	intermittent pain
dolor leve (m)	slight pain
dolor menstrual (m)	menstrual pain
dolor quemante (m)	burning pain
dolor referido (m)	referred pain
dolores (m/pl, col)	contractions
dolores de parto (m/pl)	labor pains
dolores de estómago (m/pl)	abdominal cramps
dolores de la regla (m/pl)	menstrual cramps
dolorido/dolorida (adj)	sore, tender
doloroso/dolorosa (adj)	painful, tender
donado/donada (adj)	donated
donadoro (m), donadora (f)	donor

donante (m/f)	donor
dormir (vb)	to sleep
dosificación (f)	dosage
dosis (f)	dose
dosis diaria (f)	daily dose
dosis diaria recomendada (f) (RDA)	recommended dietary allowance
dosis excesiva (f)	overdose
DPT (difteria, pertusis, tétano) (f)	DPT (diphtheria, pertussis, tetanus)
drogadicción (f)	drug addiction
drogadicto (m)/drogadicta (f)	drug addict
drogas (f/pl)	drugs (illegal)
drogas ilegales (f/pl)	illegal drugs
ducha (f)	douche, shower
ducharse (vb)	to shower
duodeno (m)	duodenum

E

eccema (m)	eczema
eczema (m)	eczema
eclampsia (f)	eclampsia
eclipsado (m)	cleft palate
ecocardiograma (m)	echocardiogram
edad (f)	age
edema (m)	edema
edema pulmonar (m)	pulmonary edema
efecto secundario (m)	side effect
ejercicio (m)	exercise
electrocardiograma (m)	electrocardiogram – EKG/ECG
electrocución (f)	electrocution
electrodos (m/pl)	electrodes
electroencefalogramo (m) EEG	electroencephalogram -
electromiograma (m)	electromyogram - EMG
elevar (vb)	to elevate
elixir (m)	elixir
embarazada (adj)	pregnant
embarazo (m)	pregnancy
embarazo cervical (m)	cervical pregnancy
embarazo ectópico (m)	ectopic pregnancy
embarazo en los tubos (m)	ectopic pregnancy
embarazo ovárico (m)	ovarian pregnancy

embarazo tubarico (m)	tubal pregnancy
embolia (f)	clot, embolism
embolia cerebral (f)	stroke
embolismo (m)	embolism
embrión (m)	embryo
emergencia (f)	emergency
empacho (m)	indigestion, constipation, ulcer
empaste (m)	dental filling
empeoramiento (m)	deterioration
enanismo (m)	dwarfism
encamado (m), encamada (f)	bedridden patient
encamorrado (adj, col)	sleepy
encefalitis (f)	encephalitis
encías (f/pl)	gums
encías sangrantes (f/pl)	bleeding gums
encinta (adj)	pregnant
endémico/endémica (adj)	endemic
endocarditis (f)	endocarditis
endocrino/endocrina (adj)	endocrine
endocrinólogo (m), endocrinóloga (f)	endocrinologist
endocrinología (f)	endocrinology
endodoncia (f)	root canal
endometrio (m)	endometrium
endometriosis (f)	endometriosis
endorfina (f)	endorphin
endoscopía (f)	endoscopy
endurecimiento (m)	hardening
enema (m)	enema
enérgico/enérgica (adj)	active
enfermedad (f)	disease, illness
enfermedad autoinmune (f)	autoimmune illness
enfermedad cardiaca coronaria (f)	coronary heart disease
enfermedad cardiovascular (f)	cardiovascular disease
enfermedad crónica (f)	chronic illness
enfermedad de Crohn (f)	Crohn's disease
enfermedad de Graves (f)	Graves Disease
enfermedad de la vesícula (f)	gall bladder disease
enfermedad de los pulmones (f)	lung disease
enfermedad de Parkinson (f)	Parkinson's disease
enfermedad del corazón (f)	heart disease
enfermedad del riñón (f)	kidney disease
enfermedad del sueño (f)	sleeping sickness
enfermedad endémica (f)	endemic illness
enfermedad epidémica (f)	epidemic illness
enfermedad de células falciformes (f)	sickle cell disease

enfermedad de transmision sexual (f)	sexually transmitted disease
enfermedad inflamatoria pélvica (f)	pelvic inflamatory disease (PID)
enfermedad mental (f)	mental illness/disease
enfermedad nerviosa (f)	nervous breakdown
enfermedad periodontal (f)	periodontal disease
enfermedad por descompresión (f)	bends
enfermedades venéreas (f/pl)	STDs, STIs, venereal disease
enfermero (m), enfermera (f)	nurse
enfermizo (m), enfermiza (f)	sickly, unhealthy
enfermo/enferma (adj)	ill, sick
enfermo de babea (m)	drooling
enficema (f)	emphysema
enflaquecimiento (m)	emaciation
enfriamiento (m, col)	old (illness)
engañado/engañada (adj)	abused, fooled
engordar (vb)	to gain weight, change weight
enjuague bucal (m)	mouthwash
enojo (m)	anger
enrojecimiento (m)	flush, redness
ensayar (vb)	to practice, test
entablillar (vb)	to splint
entorpecido/entorpecida (adj)	numb
entraña (f)	bowel
entrarle calores y fríos (vb)	chill
entrecejo (m)	space between eyebrows
entretenedor (m)	pacifier
entumecido/entumecida (adj)	numb and/or swollen
entumecimiento (m)	numbness
entumido/entumida (adj)	numb
enuresis (f)	bed-wetting
envenenamiento (m)	poisoning
envenenamiento de la sangre (m)	blood poisoning
envenenamiento por comestibles (m)	food poisoning
envenenar (vb)	to poison
enzima (f)	enzyme
epidemia (f)	epidemic
epidémico/epidémica (adj)	epidemic
epidural (adj)	epidural
epiglotis (f)	epiglottis
epilepsia (f)	epilepsy
episiotomía (f)	episiotomy
episodio de atragantamiento (m)	choking
epistaxis (f)	bloody nose
equilibrio (m)	balance
erección (f)	erection
erosión (f)	erosion
eructar (vb)	to burp

eructo (m)	belch
erupción (f)	rash
erupción del panal (f)	diaper rash
escaldadura (f)	scald
escalofríos (m/pl)	chills
escalpelo (m)	scalpel
escama (f)	scale, flake
escamoso/escamosa (adj)	scaly
escápula (f)	shoulder blade
escara (f)	scab, crust
escayola (f)	cast
esclerosis múltiple (f)	multiple sclerosis
esclerótica (f)	sclera
escolafrío (m)	shiver
escoliosis (f)	scoliosis
escorbuto (m)	scurvy
escorpión (m)	scorpion
escroto (m)	scrotum
escuchar (vb)	to listen
escupir (vb)	to spit
escupo (m)	phlegm, sputum
escurrimiento (m)	nasal discharge
esencial (adj)	essential
esfínter (m)	sphincter
esfuerzo (m)	exertion
esguince (m)	sprain, twist
esmalte (m)	enamel
esófago (m)	esophagus
espalda (f)	back, waist, lower back
espantado/espantada (adj)	scared
espantoso/espantosa (adj)	scary
espasmo (m)	spasm
espasmo muscular (m)	muscle spasm
especialista (m/f)	specialist
espécimen (m)	specimen
espectativa de vida (f)	life expectancy
espéculo (m)	speculum
espejuelos (m/pl)	eye glasses
esperma (f)	sperm, semen
espermecida (m)	spermicide
espeso/espesa (adj)	stiff, thick
espina (f)	backbone, spine
espina dorsal (f)	backbone, spine
espina bífida (f)	spina bifida
espinazo (m)	back, backbone
espinilla (f)	shin

espinillas (f/pl)	acne, blackheads
espirometria (f)	spirometry
espolón (m)	bone spur
esponja (f)	sponge
espuma (f)	foam
esputo (m)	saliva, sputum
esqueleto (m)	skeleton
esquizofrenia (f)	schizophrenia
esquizofrénico/esquizofrénica (adj)	schizophrenic
estable (adj)	stable
estado (m)	condition
estado civil (m)	marital status
estar alterado (vb)	to be anxious
estar congestionado (vb)	to be congested
estar constipado (vb)	to be congested
estar de luto (vb)	to mourn
estar deprimido (vb)	to be depressed
estar estreñido (vb)	to be constipated
estar inconsciente (vb, col)	to faint
estar mareado (vb, col)	to be dizzy
estar nervioso (vb)	to be nervous, anxious
estar obstruído (vb, col)	to be congested
estar somnoliento (vb)	to be sleepy
estar tieso (vb)	rigidity
estar vomitando (vb)	vomiting
estéril (adj)	sterile, infertile
esterilidad (f)	sterility
esterelidad femenina (f)	female sterility
esterilización (f)	sterilization
esterilizar (vb)	to sterilize
esternón (m)	sternum, breastbone
esteroide (m)	steroid
estética (f)	cosmetic surgery, face-lift
estetoscopio (m)	stethoscope
estilo de vida (m)	lifestyle
estimulante (f)	stimulant
estoma (m)	stoma
estómago (m)	stomach, belly, abdomen*
estómago revuelto (m)	nauseous feelings, upset stomach
estornudar (vb)	to sneeze
estornudo (m)	sneeze
estrabismo (m)	squint
estrangular(se) (vb)	to strangle
estrellita (f)	floater (of the eye)
estremecerse (vb)	to shiver
estreñimiento (m)	constipation
estreptococo (m)	strep

estrés (m)	stress
estría (f)	stretch mark
estribo (m)	stirrup
estrógeno (m)	estrogen
estupor (m)	stupor
éter (m)	ether
ETS (f/pl)	STDs, STIs
euforia (f)	euphoria
eutanasia (f)	euthanasia
evacuación (f)	bowel movement
evitar (vb)	to avoid
examen (m)	checkup, test, examination
examen de detección (m)	screen
examen de estrés (m)	stress test
examen de la audición (m)	hearing test
examen de la vista (m)	vision test
examen de Papanicolao (m)	Pap smear
examen de seguimiento (m)	follow-up
examen del seno (m)	breast exam
examen físico (m)	physical exam
examen ginecológico (m)	Pap smear, pelvic exam
examinación (f)	examination
examinar (vb)	to examine
excremento (m)	stool, excrement
excremento negro (m)	black stool
excremento suelto (m)	diarrhea
excusado (m)	bathroom
exfoliación (f)	exfoliation
exhalar (vb)	to exhale
expectorante (m)	expectorant
expediente (m)	file, record
expediente médico (m)	medical chart or record
experto/experta (adj)	expert
experto (m), experta (f)	expert
explicar (vb)	to explain
explorador (adj)	exploratory operation
exploratorio/exploratoria (adj)	exploratory surgery
exposición (m)	exposure
externo/externa (adj)	external
extirpacion (f)	removal
extracción (f)	extraction
extractor de leche (m)	breast pump
extraer (vb)	to extract
extraño/extraña (adj)	unusual
extremidad (f)	limb

extremidad lisiada (f)	limp, crippled/lame extremity
extremidad tullida (f)	limp, crippled/lame extremity
eyaculación (f)	ejaculation
eyacular (vb)	to ejaculate

F

factor Rhesus/RH (m)	RH factor
factores de riesgo (m/pl)	risk factors
fahrenheit (adj)	fahrenheit
fallecer (vb)	pass away
fallecido/fallecida (adj)	deceased
fallo (m)	shock
fallo cardíaco (m)	cardiac arrest
falta de aire (f, col)	shortness of breath
falta de aliento (f, col)	shortness of breath
falta de ánimo (f, col)	weakness
falta de energía (f, col)	weakness
falta de regla (f)	amenorrhea
falta de respiración (f)	shortness of breath
falta de ritmo regular (f)	arrhythmia
familia (f)	family
faringe (m)	pharynx
farmacéutico (m), farmacéutica (f)	pharmacist
farmacia (f)	pharmacy
fatal (adj)	fatal
fatiga (f)	fatigue, tiredness
fatigado/fatigada (adj)	weary
fecales (f/pl)	feces
fecha (f)	date
fecha apróximada de parto (f)	due date
fecha de nacimiento (f)	birthdate
fecha de vencimiento (f)	due date
fecundación (f)	fertilization
feliz (adj)	happy
fémur (m)	femur
fenómeno de Raynaud (m)	Raynaud's phenomenon
fértil (adj)	fertile
fertilización (f)	fertilization
fertilización en vitro (f)	in-vitro fertilization
férula (f)	splint
feto (m)	fetus
fibra (f)	fiber
fibrilación (f)	fibrillation
fibroide (m)	fibroid
fibroideo (m)	fibroid

fibrosis quística (f)	cystic fibrosis
fiebre (f)	fever
fiebre amarilla (f)	yellow fever
fiebre del heno (f)	hay fever
fiebre escarlatina (f)	scarlet fever
fiebre púrpura (f)	spotted fever
fiebre reumática (f)	rheumatic fever
fiebre tifoidea (f)	typhoid fever
filoso/filosa (adj)	sharp
filtro solar (m)	sunscreen
fino/fina (adj)	thin
físico (m)	physical exam
fisioterapia (f)	physical therapy
fisura (f)	fissure, hairline fracture
fisura del paladar (f)	cleft palate
flaco/flaca (adj)	skinny
flato (m)	gas
flatulencia (f)	flatulance
flema (f)	sputum, phlegm
flexible (adj)	flexible
flojera (f, col)	fatigue
flojo (m)	limp
flotadores (m/pl)	floaters
flujo (m)	discharge
flujo de la vagina (m)	vaginal discharge
fluoroscopia (f)	fluoroscopy
fluoruro (m)	fluoride
flúter (adj)	flutter
fobia (f)	phobia
fogajes (m/pl)	hot flashes
folleto (m)	pamphlet
folículo (m)	follicle
fontanela (f)	fontanelle
fórceps (m/pl)	forceps
fórmula (f)	formula
formulario (m)	form
fosa nasal (f)	nasal cavity, nostril
fósforo (m)	phosphorus
fotosensibilidad (f)	photosensitivity
fracaso (m)	abortion
fractura (f)	fracture
fractura compuesta (f)	compound fracture
fractura múltiple (f)	multiple fracture
fractura simple (f)	simple fracture
fracturado/fracturada (adj)	broken
frecuencia (f)	frequency

frequencia del pulso (f)	pulse rate
frenillos (m/pl)	dental braces
frenos (m/pl)	dental braces
frente (f)	forehead
fresa (f)	dentist's drill
fricción (f)	rub, massage
frigidez (f)	frigidity
frío/fría (adj)	cold
friolento/friolenta (adj)	sensitive to cold
frotar (vb)	to massage, rub
fuego (m)	fire
fuegos (m/pl)	shingles, herpes zoster
fuerte (adj)	strong
fuerza (f)	strength
fuerza de voluntad (f)	will power
fumar (vb)	to smoke
fumar tabaco (m)	smoking
funcionar (vb)	to function
furúnculos (m/pl, col)	abscesses
fusil (m)	gun

G

gafas (f/pl)	eyeglasses, spectacles
gana (f)	appetite
ganas de vomitar (f/pl)	nausea
ganglio (m)	node
ganglio linfático (m)	lymph node, lymph gland
ganglios inflamados (m/pl)	swollen glands
gangrena (f)	gangrene
gargajo (m, col)	phlegm
garganta (f)	throat
garganta inflamada (f)	sore throat
gargarizar (vb)	to gargle
garra (f, col)	nail
garrapata (f)	tick
garrotillo (m)	croup
gas (m)	gas
gas en el estomago (m)	stomach gas, bloating
gas hilarante (m)	laughing gas

gasa (f)	gauze
gastritis (f)	gastritis
gastroenterólogo(m)/gastroenteróloga	gastroenterologist
gastroenterología (f)	gastroenterology (GI)
gastrointestinal (adj)	gastrointestinal (GI)
gatear (vb)	to crawl
gaznate (m)	windpipe
gel (m)	gel
gemelo/gemela (adj)	twin
gemelo (m), gemela (f)	twin
género (m)	gender
genes (m/pl)	genes
genético/genética (adj)	genetic
genitales (m)	genitals, private parts
geriatria (m)	geriatrics
geriátrico/geriátrica (adj)	geriatric
germen (m)	germ
gestación (f)	gestation
giardia (f)	giardia
gigantismo (m)	giantism, gigantism
ginecología (f)	gynecology
ginecólogo (m), ginecóloga (f)	gynecologist
gingivitis (f)	gingivitis
glándula (f)	gland
glándula masculina (f, col)	prostate gland
glandula pituitaria (f)	pituitary gland
glándula tiroides (f)	thyroid gland
glándulas adrenales (f/pl)	adrenal glands
glaucoma (f)	glaucoma
gliburida (f)	glyburide
glicusoria (m)	glycosuria
glóbulos (m/pl)	cells
glóbulos blancos (m/pl)	white blood cells
glóbulos rojos (m/pl)	red blood cells
glucosa (f)	glucose
gluten (m)	gluten
golpe (m, col)	trauma
golpe de calor (m)	heat stroke, sunstroke*
golpe en la cabeza (m)	head injury/trauma
goma (f)	hangover
gomitar (col)	to vomit
gonorrea (f)	gonorrhea
gordo/gorda (adj)	fat, obese
gordo (m), gorda(f)	fat or obese person
gordura (f)	obesity
gota (f)	gout, gonorrhea*

gotas (f/pl)	drops
gotas para el oído (f/pl)	ear drops
gotas para los ojos (f/pl)	eye drops
goteo (m)	leakage
gotero (m)	dropper
grados centígrados (m/pl)	centigrade
grados fahrenheit (m/pl)	fahrenheit
gráfico (m)	chart
gramo (m)	gram
granitos (m/pl)	acne, blister, pimple
grano (m)	pimple, abscess
grano en el ojo (m, col)	sty
grano enterrado (m)	skin boil
granos (m/pl, col)	hives
grasa (f)	fat (in food)
grasa en las venas (f)	cholesterol
grave (adj)	serious, seriously ill, severe
greñas (f/pl)	hair
grietas en el paladar (f/pl)	cleft palate
gripe (f)	influenza
grito (m)	scream
grueso/gruesa (adj)	thick
grupo sanguíneo (m)	blood type
guante (m)	glove
guardería (f)	nursery, day care
guardería infantil (f)	day-care center
gusanos (m/pl)	parasite infestation
gusto (m)	taste

H

habitación privada (f)	private hospital room
hábito (m)	habit
habla (f)	speech
hacer ejercicio (vb)	to exercise
hacer gárgaras (vb)	to gargle
halitosis (m)	halitosis
halucinación (f)	hallucination
hambre (adj)	hungry
hambre (m)	hunger
heces (f/pl)	feces, stool
heces mucosas (f/pl)	mucous stool
helicóptero (m)	helicopter
hematoma (m)	hematoma, bruise
hembra (f)	female

hemofilia (f)	hemophilia
hemoglobina (f)	hemoglobin
hemorragia (f)	hemorrhage, bleeding
hemorragia nasal (f)	nosebleed
hemorragia vascular (f)	stroke
hemorroides (f/pl)	hemorrhoids
hepatitis (f)	hepatitis
hepatitis tipo A/B/C (f)	hepatitis A/B/C
hereditario/hereditaria (adj)	hereditary
herencia (f)	heredity
herida (f)	wound, injury
herida de bala (f)	bullet wound
herida desgarrada (f)	laceration
herido/herida (adj)	injured, wounded, hurt
herir (vb)	to injure
hermafrodita (adj)	hermaphrodite
hermafrodita (m/f)	hermaphrodite
hermano (m)/hermana (f)	sibling
hermanos siameses (m/pl)	siamese twins
hermanas siameses (f/pl)	siamese twins
hernia (f)	hernia, rupture
heroína (f)	heroin
herpes (m)	herpes, herpes zoster, shingles
herpes zoster (m)	shingles
hervor (m, col)	heartburn, wheezing
heterosexual (adj)	heterosexual
heterosexual (m/f)	heterosexual
hidratar (vb)	to hydrate
hidrofobia (f)	rabies
hiedra venenosa (f)	poison ivy
hiel (f)	gall bladder, bile
hielo (m)	ice
hierba (f)	herb
hierro (m)	iron
hígado (m)	liver
higiene (f)	hygiene
higienista dental (m/f)	dental hygientist
hijo (m)/hija(f) de crianza	foster child
hilo dental (m)	dental floss
himen (m)	hymen
hinchado/hinchada (adj)	puffy, bloated, swollen
hinchar (vb)	to swell
hinchazón (f)	swelling
hiperacidez (f)	hyperacidity
hiperactivo/hiperactiva (adj)	hyperactive

hiperglucemia (f)	hyperglycemia
hipermétrope (adj)	farsighted
hipernatremia (f)	hypernatremia
hiperópico (m)	farsighted, hyperopic
hipersensibilidad (f)	hypersensitivity
hipertensión (f)	hypertension
hipertermia (f)	hyperthermia
hipertiroidismo (m)	hyperthyroidism
hiperventilación (f)	hyperventilation
hipo (m)	hiccups
hipocondria (f)	hypochondria
hiponatremia (f)	hyponatremia
hipotálamo (m)	hypothalamus
hipotermia (f)	hypothermia
hipotiroidismo (m)	hypothyroidism
hipoglucemia (f)	hypoglycemia
hipoxia (f)	hypoxia
hisopo (m)	cotton swab
histerectomía (f)	hysterectomy
histeria (f)	hysteria
histerismo (m)	hysteria
historia clínica (f)	medical history
hoja clínica (f)	chart
hombre (m)	man
hombro (m)	shoulder
hombro congelado (m)	frozen shoulder
homeopatía (f)	homeopathy
homosexual (adj)	homosexual
homosexual (m/f)	homosexual
hongo (m)	fungus, mushroom
hongos en los pies (m/pl)	athlete's foot
hongos venenosos (m/pl)	fly agaric, toadstool
hormigueo (m)	tingling
hormona (f)	hormone
hormona estimulante para el folículo (FSH)	follicle stimulating hormone
hormona tiroidea sintética (f)	synthetic thyroid hormone
hormonal (adj)	hormonal
hospital (m)	hospital
hospital psiquiátrico (m)	psychiatric hospital
huérfano(m), huérfana (f)	orphan
hueso (m)	bone
hueso del cuello (m, col)	collarbone
hueso del pecho (m, col)	breastbone
hueso fracturado (m)	broken bone
hueso golpeado (m)	bruised bone
hueso magullado (m)	bruised bone

hueso quebrado (m)	broken bone
hueso roto (m)	broken bone
huesos (m/pl, col)	skeleton, vertebrae
huesos del sacro (m/pl, col)	sacrum bones
huesos zafados (m/pl, col)	dislocation
huevo (m)	egg
humano (adj)	human
humano (m)	human
humo (m)	fumes, smoke

I

ibuprofén (m)	ibuprofen
ictericia (f)	jaundice
idea fija (f)	obsession
ijar (m, col)	side
imagen por resonancia magnética (f)	magnetic resonance imaging - MRI
impactación (f)	impaction
impedimento (m)	handicap
el impétigo	impetigo
implantación (f)	implantation
implantar (vb)	to implant
implante (m)	implant
impotencia (f)	impotence
impregnación (f)	impregnation
imprescindible (adj)	essential
inanición (f)	starvation
incapacidad (f)	handicap, disability
incapacitado/incapacitada (adj)	handicapped, disabled
incendio (m)	fire
incesto (m)	incest
incisión (f)	incision
incisivo (m)	incisor
incomodidad (f)	discomfort
incómodo/incómoda (adj)	uncomfortable
inconsciente (adj)	unconscious
incontinencia (f)	incontinence
incontinencia de heces (f)	fecal incontinence
incubadora (f)	incubator
incurable (adj)	incurable
índice de masa corporal (m)	body mass index
indiferencia (f)	lethargy
indigestión (f)	indigestion
inducir (vb)	to induce

inestable (adj)	unstable
infancia (f)	infancy, childhood
infante (m)	infant
infarto del corazón (m)	myocardia infarction, heart attack
infección (f)	infection
infección de la orina (f)	urinary tract infection
infección de la piel (f)	skin infection
infección de la sangre (f, col)	syphilis
infección de los oídos (f)	ear infection
infección del oído medio (f)	middle ear infection
infección de los riñones (f)	kidney infection
infección de vejiga (f)	bladder infection
infección estreptocóccica (f)	streptococcal infection
infección parasitaria (f)	parasitic infection
infección por hongos (f)	fungal/yeast infection
infección por relaciones sexuales (f)	STDs/STIs
infección vírica (f)	herpes
infectado/infectada (adj)	infected
infectar (vb)	to infect
infeliz (adj)	unhappy
infertilidad (f)	infertility
inflado (adj)	puffy
inflamación (f)	swelling, inflammation
inflamado/inflamada (adj)	inflamed, swollen
influenza (f)	influenza, flu
ingerir (vb)	to ingest
ingle (f)	groin
ingresar (vb)	to hospitalize
inhalar (vb)	to inhale
inhalador (m)	inhaler
inicio (m)	onset
injerto (m)	graft
injerto cutáneo (m)	skin graft
inmaduro/immadura (adj)	immature
inmoglubina (f)	immunoglobulin
inmóvil (adj)	immobile
inmovilización (f)	immobilization
inmune (adj)	immune
inmunidad (f)	immunity
inmunización (f)	vaccine, immunization
inmunizar (vb)	to immunize
inmunológico/inmunológica (adj)	immune
inoculación (f)	inoculation
inocular (vb)	to inoculate
inodoro (m)	toilet
inofensivo/inofensiva (adj)	harmless
insalubre (adj)	unhealthy

insecticida (m)	insecticide
insecto (m)	insect
inseminación (f)	insemination
inseminación artificial (f)	artificial insemination
insensibilidad (f)	unconsciousness
insertar (vb)	to insert
insolación (f)	heat stroke, sunstroke
insomnio (m)	insomnia
instrumento (m)	instrument
insuficiencia (f)	insufficiency
insuficiencia cardíaca (f)	heart failure
insuficiencia renal (f)	renal or kidney failure
insulina (f)	insulin
internal (adj)	internal
internar (vb)	to hospitalize, to admit
internista (m/f)	internist
interno (adj)	internal
intérprete (m/f)	interpreter
intersticial (adj)	interstitial
intestino (m)	intestine, gut, bowel
intestino delgado (m)	small intestine
intestino grueso (m)	large intestine
intestino mayor (m, col)	colon
intolerancia a la lactosa (f)	lactose intolerance
intoxicación (f)	poisoning, intoxication
intoxicado/intoxicada (adj)	intoxicated
(no) intoxicado (adj)	sober
intravenoso/intravenosa (adj)	intravenous (I.V.)
introducir (vb)	to insert
intubación (f)	intubation
inválido/inválida (adj)	invalid, disabled
invalid (m), inválida (f)	disabled person
inyección (f)	injection, shot
inyección contra el tétano (f)	tetanus shot
inyección de refuerzo (f)	booster shot
inyectar (vb)	to inject
ipecacuana (f)	ipecac
irrigación nasal (f)	nasal irrigation
irrigar (vb)	to irrigate
irritación (f)	rash, irritation
isquemia cerebral (f)	cerebral ischemia
izquierda (adj)	left, left-handed

J

---

jabón (m)	soap
jadear (vb)	to pant
jadeo (m)	panting, wheezing, gasping
jalea (f)	jelly
jaqueca (f)	migraine
jarabe (m)	syrup
jarabe para la tos (m)	cough syrup
jeringa (f)	syringe
jeringuilla (f)	syringe
jiotes (m/pl)	fungal infection
jorobado/jorobada (adj)	hunchback
jorobado (m), /jorobada (f)	hunchback
juanete (m)	bunion
jugo (m)	juice
jugo gástrico (m)	gastric juice

K

kilogramo	kilogram

L

laberintitis (f)	labyrinthitis
labio leporino (m)	cleft palate
labios (m/pl)	lips
laboratorio (m)	laboratory
laceración (f)	laceration
laceración del perineo (f)	laceration of the perineum
lactancia (f)	lactation
lactar (vb)	to breastfeed, lactate
lactosa (f)	lactose
ladillas (f/pl)	crabs
lado (m)	side
lágrima (f)	tear, teardrop
lamentar (vb)	to mourn
languidez (f)	listlessness
laparascopía (f)	laparoscopy
laringe (f)	larynx
laringitis (f)	laryngitis
lastimado/lastimada (adj)	hurt
lastimadura (f)	injury, sprain, dislocation, muscle pull

lastimar (vb)	to injure
latente (adj)	pulsating
látex (m)	latex
latido (m)	hunger pang, throb
latido del corazón (m)	heartbeat
latidos (m/pl, col)	palpitations
latidos cardíacos irregulares (m/pl)	irregular heartbeat
latidos cardíacos rápidos (m/pl)	rapid heartbeat
lavado de vagina (m)	douche
lavado intestinal (m)	enema
lavar (vb)	to wash
lavativa (f)	enema
laxante (m)	laxative
lazarín (m, col)	leprosy
leche de magnesia (f)	milk of magnesia
leche materna (f)	breast milk
leer los labios (vb)	to lipread
lengua (f)	tongue
lenguaje (m)	language
lentes (m/pl)	glasses, contact lenses
lentes de contacto (m/pl)	contact lenses
lepra (f)	leprosy
lesbiana (f)	lesbian
lesión (f)	lesion, wound, injury
lesión de latigazo (f)	whiplash
lesión por golpe (f)	contusion
lesionado/lesionada (adj)	injured
letargo (m)	lethargy
leucemia (f)	leukemia
libido (f)	libido
libra (f)	pound (weight)
ligadura (f)	tourniquet
ligadura de trompas (f)	tubal ligation
ligamento (m)	ligament
ligar las trompas (vb)	to tie tubes
linfa (f)	lymph
linfoma (m)	lymphoma
linimento (m)	liniment
liposucción (f)	liposuction
líquido (adj)	liquid
liquido amniótico (m)	amniotic fluid
líquido cefalorraquídeo (m)	spinal fluid
líquidos intravenosos (m/pl)	intravenous fluids
lisiado/lisiada (adj)	crippled, limp
lisiado (m), lisiada (f)	crippled or handicapped person
lisiar (vb)	to cripple

llaga (f)	sore, wound, ulcer
llaga de cama (f)	bed sore
lleno de sangre (adj)	engorged
llevar luto (vb)	to mourn
llorar (vb)	to cry, mourn
lobotomía (f)	lobotomy
lóbulo (m)	lobe
lóbulo de la oreja (m)	earlobe
loción (f)	lotion
loco/loca (adj)	insane
locura (f)	insanity, mental illness
lombrices (f/pl)	parasite infestation
lombriz intestinal (f)	tapeworm, intestinal worm
lomo (m, col)	loin, lower back
LSD dietilamida del ácido lisérgico (f)	Lysergic acid diethylamide - LSD
lubricante (m)	lubricant
lubricante vaginal (m)	vaginal lubricant
lubricar (vb)	to lubricate
lucha (f)	fight
lucidez (f)	sanity
lugar de nacimiento (m)	place of birth
lumpectomía (f)	lumpectomy
lunar (m)	birthmark, mole
lunares (m/pl)	blemishes
lupus (m)	lupus
luz (f)	light

M

macho (adj)	male
madre subrogada (f)	surrogate mother
madurez (f)	maturity
magulladura (f)	bruise
mal (m)	sickness
mal aliento (m)	halitosis, bad breath
mal de la cabeza (m, col)	headache
mal de minero (m)	hookworm
mal de montaña (m)	mountain sickness
mal de pecho (m, col)	asthma
mal de Hansen (m, col)	leprosy
mal de San Lázaro (m, col)	leprosy
mal del apendis (m, col)	appendicitis
mal del corazón (m, col)	heart attack
mal del ojo (m, col)	conjunctivitis
mala circulación (f)	poor circulation
mala sangre (f, col)	syphilis

malabsorción (f)	malabsorption
malaria (f, col)	malaria
malestar (m)	malaise
malestar general (m)	general malaise
malestares de la mañana (m/pl)	morning sickness
malformación (f)	malformation
maligno/maligna (adj)	malignant
malnutrición (f)	malnutrition
malo/mala (adj)	sick, bad
malogro (m)	abortion
malparto (m)	miscarriage
mamadera (f)	baby bottle
mamografía (f)	mammogram
mamograma (m)	mammogram
mancha de nacimiento (f, col)	birthmark
manchado de sangre por la vagina (m)	spotting
manchar (vb)	to stain
manchas (f/pl)	spots, blemishes
mandíbula (f)	jaw
manguera (f)	tube
manía (f)	mania
maníaco/maníaca (adj)	manic
maníaco-depresivo/depresiva (adj)	manic-depressive
maniáco (m/f)	maniac
manicomio (m)	mental hospital
mano (f)	hand
manos frías (f/pl)	cold hands
manos húmedas (f/pl)	cold hands
manteca (f)	heroin
mantener (vb)	to support
manzanilla (f)	chamomile
marasmo (m)	consumption
marcador de ritmo (m)	pacemaker
marcapaso (m)	pacemaker
marcas de viruelas (f/pl)	pocks
mareado/mareada (adj)	dizzy, groggy
mareador (adj)	dazed
marearse (vb)	to become dizzy
mareo (m)	light-headedness, daze
mareo (en un barco) (m)	seasickness
mareos (m/pl)	dizziness
marijuana (f)	marijuana
martillo de reflejos (m)	reflex hammer
masa (f)	lump, mass
masa de mama (f)	breast mass
masaje (m)	massage

masajear (vb)	to massage, rub
masas de los senos (f/pl)	breast masses
mascar (vb)	to chew
máscara (f)	mask
mascarilla (f)	respirator
masculine (adj)	male
masculino (adj)	male
mastectomía (f)	mastectomy
masticar (vb)	to chew
matar (vb)	to kill
matarse (vb)	to commit suicide
materia fecal (f)	feces
material de contraste (m)	contrast material
materno/materna (adj)	maternal
matriz (f)	womb, uterus*
mechón (m)	patch
medicamento (m)	medicine, medication
medicamentos de venta libre (m/pl) OTC	over–the-counter medication –
medicamentos genericos (m/pl)	generic drugs
medicina (f)	medicine
medicina de receta (f)	prescription
medicinar (vb)	to medicate
medico (m), médica (f)	doctor, physician
medico (m), médica (f) de guardia	doctor-on-call
medio ambiente (m)	environment
médula (f)	bone marrow
médula espinal (f)	spinal cord
médula ósea (f)	bone marrow
mejilla (f)	cheek
mejorar (vb)	to improve
melanoma (m)	melanoma
melena (f)	melena
mellizos/mellizas (adj)	twin
mellizos (m), mellizas (f)	twins
membrane (f)	membrane
memoria (f)	memory
meningitis (f)	meningitis
menopausia (f)	menopause
menstruación (f) period	menstruation, monthly
menstruar (vb)	to menstruate
mente (f)	mind
mentón (m)	chin
merienda (f)	snack
mesa (f)	table
mesa de operaciones (f)	operating table

metabolismo (m)	metabolism
metabolizar (vb)	to metabolize
metadona (f)	methadone
metanfetamina (f)	methamphetamine
metástasis del cáncer (f)	metastasis
meter (vb)	to insert
método de Lamaze (m)	Lamaze Method
método del ritmo (m)	rhythm method
mezquino (m, col)	wart
microcirugía (f)	microsurgery
microorganismo (m)	microorganism
microscopio (m)	microscope
miedo (m)	fear
miembro (m)	limb
migraña (f, col)	migraine
mineral (m)	mineral
minusválido/minusválida (adj)	handicapped
miopía (f)	myopia, nearsightedness
moco (m)	mucus, phlegm, nasal discharge
modo de vida (m)	lifestyle
modorra (f)	drowsiness
modos de conducta (m/pl)	behavior patterns
moisés (m/pl)	bassinet
mojar (vb)	to lubricate
mojo (m)	mold, mildew
molar (m)	molar
moler (vb)	to grind, crush
molestar (vb)	to bother, molest
molestia (f)	complaint, trouble, earache
molestia abdominal (f)	abdominal discomfort
molestias en el pecho (f/pl)	chest discomfort
molestia estomacal (f)	upset stomach
mollera (f)	fontanelle
mollera caída (f)	fallen fontanelle
monga (f)	flu
monitor (m)	monitor
monitorear (vb)	to monitor
monitoreo (m)	monitor
monitoreo fetal (m)	fetal monitor
mononucleosis (f)	mononucleosis
mononucleosis infecciosa (f)	mononucleosis
moquera (f, col)	nasal discharge
morado (m, col)	bruise
mordedura (f)	bite

mordedura de garrapata (f)	tick bite
mordedura de serpiente (f)	snakebite
mordedura humana (f)	human bite
mordida (f)	bite
mordida de perro (f)	dog bite
morete (m, col)	bruise
moreteado/moreteada (adj)	bruised
moretón (m)	bruise
morfina (f)	morphine
morgue (f)	morgue
morir (vb)	to die
mortal (adj)	fatal
mortalidad (f)	mortality
mosquito (m)	mosquito
mota (f)	mite
movimiento (m)	movement
movimiento de los intestinos (m)	bowel movement
mucosidad (f)	mucus, nasal discharge
mucoso/mucosa (adj)	mucous
mudo/muda (adj)	mute
mudo (m), muda (f)	mute person
muela (f)	molar
muela del juicio (f)	wisdom tooth
muerte (f)	death
muerte cerebral (f)	brain dead
muerte fetal (f)	stillbirth
muerto/muerta (adj)	dead
muerto (m), muerta (f)	corpse, dead person
muestra (f)	sample, specimen
muestra de heces (f)	stool specimen
muestra de orina (f)	urine sample
muestra de sangre (f)	blood smear
mujer (f)	woman
mujercita (f, col)	female
muletas (f/pl)	crutches
muñeca (f)	wrist
murmullo (m, col)	heart murmur
músculo (m)	muscle
músculo cardíaco (m)	cardiac muscle
músculo golpeado (m)	bruised muscle
músculo magullado (m)	bruised muscle
músculo rasgado (m)	pulled muscle
muslo (m)	thigh
mutación (f)	mutation
muy fuerte (adj)	severe

nacer (vb)	to be born
nacido (m)	skin boil
nacido muerto (m)	stillborn
nacidos (m/pl, col)	abscesses
nacimiento (m)	birth
nacimiento prematuro (m)	premature birth
nacimiento postumo (m)	afterbirth
nalga (f)	buttock
narcolepsia (f)	narcolepsy
narcótico (m)	narcotic
narcotraficante (m/f)	drug-seller
narices (f/pl)	nostrils
nariz (f)	nose, nostril
nariz constipada (f)	nasally congested
nariz mocosa (f)	runny nose
nariz tapada (f)	stuffy nose, nasally congested
natalidad (f)	birth
natural (adj)	natural
náusea (f)	nausea
náuseas matutinas (f)	morning sickness
nauseabundo/nauseabunda (adj)	nauseating, quesy
nebulizador (m)	nebulizer
necesidad (f)	need
necesitar (vb)	to need
nefritis (f)	nephritis
negligencia médica (f)	malpractice
nene (m), nena (f)	child, baby
neonatal (adj)	neonatal
neoplasia (f)	tumor
neoplasma (m)	tumor
nervio (m)	nerve
nervioso/nerviosa (adj)	nervous
neumología (f)	pulmonology
neumonía (f)	pneumonia
neumonía doble (f)	double pneumonia
neuralgia (f)	neuralgia
neurasthenia (f)	neurasthenia
neuritis (f)	neuritis
neurocirujano (m)	neurosurgeon
neurología (f)	neurology
neurólogo (m), neuróloga (f)	neurologist
neurosis (f)	neurosis
neurótico/neurótica (adj)	neurotic
neurotico (m), neurótica (f)	neurotic person

nicotina (f)	nicotine
niña del ojo (f, col)	pupil
niñez (f)	childhood
nitroglicerina (f)	nitroglycerine
nocivo/nociva (adj)	harmful
nodo (m)	node
nodriza (f)	wet nurse
nódulo (m)	node, lump
nombrar (vb)	to name
nombre (m)	name
normal (adj)	normal
nostalgia del hogar (f)	homesickness
novocaína (f)	novocaine
nube del ojo (f, col)	cataract
nuca (f)	nape, neck, back of neck
nudillo (m)	knuckle
nudo (m)	knot
nuez de Adán (f)	Adam's apple
nuez de la garganta (f)	Adam's apple
nutricio (m)	nutrient
nutrición (f)	nutrition, nourishment
nutriólogo (m), nutrióloga (f)	nutritionist
nutrir (vb)	to nurture

O

obesidad (f)	obesity
obeso/obesa (adj)	obese
obrar (vb)	to defecate, have a bowel movement
observación (f)	observation
obsesión (f)	obsession
obstetra (m/f)	obstetrician
obstetricia (f)	obstetrics
obstetricia y ginecología (f) OB/GYN	Obstetrics/Gynecology –
obstrucción (f)	blockage, obstruction, block
oclusión (f)	occlusion
oclusión de una arteria (f)	arterial occlusion
odontalgia (f)	toothache
odontología (f)	dentistry
odontólogo (m), odontóloga (f)	dentist
oficina (f)	office
oftalmía contagiosa/rosada (f)	pinkeye
oftalmología (f)	ophtalmology
oftalmólogo (m), oftalmóloga (f)	ophthalmologist

oído (m)	inner ear
oído medio (m)	middle ear
oído, nariz, y garganta	ear, nose, and throat (ENT)
oír (vb)	to hear
ojo (m)	eye
ojo perezoso (m)	lazy eye
ojos bizcos (m/pl)	crossed eyes
ojos cansados (m/pl)	eye strain
ojos fatigados (m/pl)	eye strain
ojos llorosos (m/pl)	watery eyes
ojos secos (m/pl)	dry eyes
oler (vb)	to smell
olor (m)	odor, smell
ombligo (m)	navel, belly button
omóplato (m)	shoulder blade, scapula
oncología (f)	oncology
oncólogo (m), oncóloga (f)	oncologist
orina opaca (f)	cloudy urine
operación (f)	operation, surgery
operación cesárea (f)	cesarean section/operation
operación exploratoria (f)	exploratory operation
operar (vb)	to operate
opio (m)	opium
óptico/óptica (adj)	optic
óptico(m), óptica (f)	optician
optometrista (m/f)	optometrist
oral (adj)	oral
oreja (f)	outer ear
órgano (m)	organ
órganos reproductivos (m/pl)	reproductive organs
órgano vital (m)	vital organ
orgasmo (m)	orgasm
orificio (m)	orifice
orina (f)	urine
orinal (m)	bedpan, urinal
orinar (vb)	to urinate
órolo (m)	mite
ortodoncia (f)	orthodontics
ortodoncista (m/f)	orthodontist
ortopedia (f)	orthopedics
ortopedista (m/f)	orthopedist
orzuelo (m)	sty
osteoartritis (f)	osteoarthritis
osteópata (m/f)	osteopath
osteoporisis (f)	osteoporosis
otitis (f)	otitis

otorrinolaringólogo (m)	otolaryngologist
ovario (m)	ovary
ovulación (f)	ovulation
ovular (vb)	to ovulate
óvulo (m)	egg
oxígeno (m)	oxygen

P

paciente (m/f)	patient
paciente externo(m)/externa (f)	outpatient
paciente hospitalizado (m)	inpatient
paciente hospitalizada (f)	inpatient
paciente interno (m)/interna (f)	inpatient
padecer (vb)	to suffer
padecimiento (m)	ailment
padrastro (m)	hangnail
paladar (m)	palate
paladar hendido (m)	cleft palate
paleta (f, col)	shoulder blade
palidez (f)	paleness
palidéz de la cara (f)	face paleness
pálido/pálida (adj)	pale
palma (f)	palm
palma de la mano (f)	palm
palpitacíon (f)	palpitation
paludismo (m)	malaria
pañal (m)	diaper
pañalitis (f)	diaper rash
páncreas (m)	pancreas
pancreatitis ictericia (f)	jaundice pancreatitis
paño (m)	skin discoloration
pantorrilla (f)	calf (of leg)
pañuelo de papel (m)	tissue paper
pañuelo desechable (m)	tissue paper
panza (f)	belly, stomach
paperas falfallota (f/pl)	mumps
papila gustativa (f)	taste bud
parálisis (f)	paralysis, palsy
parálisis cerebral (f)	cerebral palsy
parálisis facial (f)	facial paralysis
parálisis infantil (f)	infantile paralysis
paralítico/paralítica (adj)	paralyzed
paramédico (m), paramédica (f)	paramedic
paranoia (f)	paranoia
paranoico/paranoica (adj)	paranoid

parapléjico/parapléjica (adj)	paraplegic
parapléjico (m), parapléjica (f)	paraplegic
parásito (m)	parasite
parasitosis (f)	parasite infestation
parche (m)	patch
pariente consanguineo (m)	blood relative
parir (vb)	to deliver a baby
paro cardiac (m)	cardiac arrest
parótidas (f/pl)	mumps
parpadear (vb)	to blink
párpado (m)	eyelid
partera (f)	midwife
partes (f/pl)	genitals
partes privadas (f/pl)	genitals
partes genitales (f/pl)	genitalia
partidura (f, col)	dryness
parto (m)	childbirth, child delivery
parto de nalgas (m)	breech delivery
parto inducido (m)	induced labor
parto natural (m)	natural childbirth
pasar gas (vb)	to pass gas
pasta de dientes (f)	toothpaste
pastilla (f)	pill, tablet, lozenge
pastilla anticonceptiva (f)	birth control pill
pastilla para el dolor (f)	painkiller
pastillas para la tos (f/pl)	cough drops, lozenges
pata (f, col)	leg
paterno/paterna (adj)	paternal
patizambo (m)	clubfoot
pato (m)	bedpan, urinal
patólogo (m), patóloga (f)	pathologist
peca (f)	freckle
pecho (m)	chest, breast
pediatra (m/f)	pediatrician
pediatría (f)	pediatrics
pediátrico/pediátrica (adj)	pediatric
pedo (m, col)	gas
pelea (f)	fight
pelear (vb)	to fight
peligro (m)	danger
peligroso/peligrosa (adj)	dangerous
pellojo (m, col)	facial skin
pelo (m)	hair
pelo aceitoso (m)	oily hair
pelo grasoso (m)	oily hair
pelón (adj)	bald

peluca (f)	wig
pelvis (f)	pelvis
pena (f)	grief, ache
pene (m)	penis
penetrar (vb)	to penetrate
penicilina (f)	penecillin
peor (adv, adj)	worse
perder el conocimiento (vb)	to faint, lose consciousness
perder los sentidos (vb)	to faint, lose consciousness
pérdida (f)	miscarriage
pérdida de peso (f)	weight loss
pérdida de sangre (f)	blood loss
pérdida del conocimiento (f)	unconsciousness
perforación (f)	perforation
perforación del tímpano (f)	eardrum perforation
perico (m)	cocaine
perilla (f, col)	sty
perineo (m)	perineum
período (m)	menstruation, menstrual period, menses
periodo de incubación (m)	incubation period
periodos de calor y frio (m/pl)	hot and cold spells
perjudicar (vb)	to harm
perjudicial (adj)	harmful
perlesía (f)	palsy
peroné (m)	fibula
peróxido de hidrógeno (m)	hydrogen peroxide
perro guía (m)	seeing eye dog
pesadez (f, col)	fatigue
pesadilla (f)	nightmare
pesar (vb)	to weigh
pesar (m)	grief
pescuezo (m, col)	neck
peso (m)	weight
pestaña (f)	eyelash
peste bubónica (f)	bubonic plague
peste cristal (f, col)	chicken pox
pezón (m)	nipple
pezón invertido (m)	inverted nipple
pezuña (f, col)	nail
picada (f, col)	sting
picado/picada (adj)	decayed
picadura (f)	cavity, puncture, insect sting
picadura de abeja (f)	bee sting
picadura de araña (f)	spider bite

picadura de insecto (f)	insect sting
picar (vb)	to sting, prick, itch
picazón (f)	itching, itch
pie (m)	foot
pie de atleta (m)	athlete's foot
pie plano (m)	flat foot
piedras biliares (f/pl)	gallstones
piedras en los riñones (f/pl)	kidney stones
piel (f)	skin
piel aceitosa (f)	oily skin
piel grasosa (f)	oily skin
piel agrietada (f)	chapped skin
piel amarilla (f)	yellow skin, jaundice
piel de gallina (f)	goose bumps
piel rajada (f)	chapped skin
piel reseca (f)	dry skin
piel seca (f)	dry skin
pierna (f)	leg
piernas corvas (f/pl)	bowed legs
piernas inquietas (f/pl)	restless legs
piernas zambas (f/pl)	bowed legs
píldora (f)	birth control pill, pill
píldora para dormir (f)	sleeping pill
pinchazo (m)	puncture
pinzas (f/pl)	forceps, tweezers, pliers
piocha (f, col)	chin
piojos (m/pl)	lice
piojos de la cabeza (m/pl)	head lice
piojos pegadizos (m/pl)	pubic lice
piojos públicos (m/pl)	pubic lice
piorrea (f)	pyorrhea
piquete (m)	puncture, sting
piquiña (f, col)	itching
pirosis (f)	heartburn
pirulas (f/pl, col)	amphetamines
pisa-lengua (f)	tongue depressor
pistola (f)	gun
piuria (f)	pyuria
placa (f)	plaque, dental plate
placenta (f)	placenta, afterbirth
plaga (f)	plague
plaga bubónica (f)	bubonic plague
plan de alimentación (m)	eating plan
plan de tratamiento (m)	treatment plan
planificación familiar (f)	family planning
planta del pie (f)	sole (of the foot)

plantillo (m, col)	calf (of the leg)
plaqueta (f)	platelet
plaqueta de sangre (f)	blood platelet
plasma (m)	plasma
pleuresía (f)	pleurisy
plomo (m)	lead
pneumonía (f)	pneumonia
podagra (f)	gout
podiatra (m/f)	podiatrist
polen (m)	pollen
policía (f)	police
polio (m)	polio
poliomelitis (f)	polio
pólipo (m)	polyp
poliuria (f)	polyuria
polvo (m)	dust, powder
pomada (f)	ointment, salve
poner en cuarentena (vb)	to quarantine
poner puntos (vb)	to stitch
ponerse de pie (vb)	to stand
ponzoñoso/ponzoñosa (adj)	poisonous
por vena (adv)	I.V.
por vía bucal (adv)	orally
por vía oral (adv)	orally
poro (m)	pore
postema (m)	abscess
postemilla (f)	canker sore
postilla (f)	scab
postizo/postiza (adj)	prosthetic
postmenopaúsico (adj)	postmenopausal
postparto (adj)	postpartum
postración (f)	heat stroke
postración nerviosa (f)	nervous breakdown
potasio (m)	potassium
potencia (f)	strength
potente (adj)	strong
practicante (m)	orderly
practicar exámenes de detección (vb)	to screen
predisponer (vb)	to predispose
predispuesto/predispuesta (adj)	predisposed
preeclampsia (f)	preeclampsia
pregunta (f)	question
premenopáusico/premenopáusica (adj)	premenopausal
premolar (f)	bicuspid
preñada (adj)	pregnant
preocupado/preocupada (adj)	worried
prepucio (m)	foreskin

presbicia (f)	presbyopia
presentación de nalgas (f)	breech presentation
presentación pélvica (f)	breech presentation
preservativo (m)	condom
presión (f)	pressure
presión alta (f)	hypertension, high blood pressure
presión arterial (f)	blood pressure
presión arterial alta (f)	hypertension
presión baja (f)	low blood pressure
presión de la sangre (f)	blood pressure
presión en el pecho (f)	chest tightness/pressure
presión ortostática (f)	orthostatic blood pressure
prevención (f)	prevention
prevenir (vb)	to prevent
primeros auxilios (m/pl)	first aid
probar (vb)	to test
probeta (f)	test tube
problemas (m/pl)	problems
problemas respiratorios (m/pl)	breathing problems
procedimiento (m)	procedure
procedimiento quirúrgico (m)	surgical procedure/operation
proctología (f)	proctology
proctólogo (m/f)	proctologist
progesterona (f)	progesterone
prolapso del recto (m)	rectal prolapse
pronóstico (m)	prognosis
pronto (adv)	quickly
propenso al vómito (m)	queasy
próstata (f)	prostate gland
protector bucal (m)	mouthpiece
protector solar (m)	sunscreen
proteína (f)	protein
prótesis (f)	prosthesis
protésico/protésica (adj)	prosthetic
protético/protética (adj)	prosthetic
protuberancia (f)	bump
proveedor de atención primaria(m)	primary care provider - PCP
prueba (f)	test
prueba de detección (f)	screening test
prueba de esfuerzo (f)	stress test
prueba de factor reumatoide (f)	rheumatoid factor test
prueba de función pulmonary (f)	pulmonary function test
prueba de la columna vertebral (f)	spinal test
prueba de sangre (f)	blood test
prueba de SIDA (f)	AIDS test
prueba de tuberculina (f)	tuberculin test

prueba del embarazo (f)	pregnancy test
prueba física (f)	physical exam
prueba para alergias (f)	allergy test
pruebas de glucosa (f/pl)	glucose tests
psicoanálisis (m)	psychoanalysis
psicología (f)	psychology
psicólogo (m)/psicóloga (f)	psychologist
psicosis (m)	psychosis
psicoterapia (f)	psychotherapy
psicótico/psicótica (adj)	psychotic
psiquiatra (m/f)	psychiatrist
psiquiatría (f)	psychiatry
psoríasis (f)	psoriasis
pubertad (f)	puberty
pujar (vb)	to push
pulga (f)	flea
pulgar (m)	thumb
pulmon (m)	lung
pulmonar (adj)	pulmonary
pulmonía (f)	pneumonia
pulmonía doble (f)	double pneumonia
pulsante (adj)	throbbing
pulsativo/pulsativa (adj)	pulsating
pulso (m)	pulse, throb
pulso irregular (m)	irregular pulse
puñalada (f)	stab
punción (f)	puncture
punción lumbar (f)	spinal tap
puño (m)	fist
puntada (f)	suture, stitch, flank pain*
puntos de suturas (m/pl)	stitches
pupa (f, col.)	blood
pupila (f)	pupil
purga (f)	laxative, purge
purgante (m)	laxative, purge
pus (m)	pus
pustule (f)	pustule

Q

que crea hábito (adj)	habit-forming
que no requiere receta médica (adj)	over-the-counter medicine
quebrado/quebrada (adj)	broken
quebradura (f)	fracture
quebrar (vb)	to break
quebrarse (vb, col)	herniate

quedarse en cama (vb)	stay in bed
queja (f)	complaint
quemadura (f)	burn
quemadura por el sol (f)	sunburn
quieto/quieta (adj)	quiet
quijada (f, col)	jaw
químico/química (adj)	chemical
químicos para el hoga (m/pl)	household chemicals
quimoterapia (f)	chemotherapy
quinina (f)	quinine
quiropráctico (m)/quiropráctica (f)	chiropractor
quirúrgico/quirúrgica (adj)	surgical
quiste (m)	cyst
quiste de ovario (m)	ovarian cyst
quitar(se) (vb)	to remove
quitarse la vida (vb)	to commit suicide

R

rabadilla (f, col)	coccyx
rabia (f)	rabies
radiaciones (m/pl)	radiation treatment
radiografía (f)	radiography
radiografía del tórax (f)	chest x-ray
radiografías (f/pl)	x-rays
radiología (f)	radiology
radiólogo (m)/radióloga (f)	radiologist
radioterapia (f)	radiotherapy
rajaduras (f/pl, col)	dryness
rápidamente (adv)	quickly
rápido (adj)	quickly
raquitismo (m)	rickets
raro/rara (adj)	unusual
rasguño (m)	scratch, scrape
raspadura (f)	abrasion
raspón (m)	scrape, abrasion, scratch
rasquera (f, col)	itching
rasurar(se) (vb)	to shave
rayos equis (m/pl)	x-rays
rayos X (m/pl)	x-rays
reacción (f)	reaction
reacción adverse (f)	adverse reaction
reacciones alérgicas (f/pl)	allergic reactions
reacción anafiláctica (f)	anaphylactic reaction
reacciones alérgicas al polvo (f/pl)	dust allergies

reactivación (f)	booster shot
readmitir (vb)	to readmit
reanimación (f)	resuscitation
reanimación cardiopulmonar (f) CPR	cardiopulmonary resuscitation -
reanimar(se) (vb)	to revive
recaída (f)	relapse
recepcionista (m/f)	receptionist
receta (f)	prescription
receta médica (f)	medical prescription
recetar (vb)	to prescribe
rechazar (vb)	to reject
recién nacido (m)/nacida (f)	newborn, neonatal
recomendación (f)	referral, recommendation
recomendar (vb)	to recommend
reconocer (vb)	to admit
reconocimiento (m)	checkup
reconocimiento de la próstata (m)	prostate examination
reconocimiento pélvico (m)	pelvic examination
reconstruir (vb)	to reconstruct
recto (m)	rectum
recuento globular (m)	blood count
recuento de globulos blancos (m)	white blood count - WBC
recuento de globulos rojos (m)	red blood count – RBC
recuento sanguíneo complete (m) CBC	complete blood count -
recuperación (f)	recovery, recuperation
recuperarse (vb)	to recover, recuperate
reemplazar (vb)	to replace
reflejo (m)	reflex
reflexión (f)	cogitation
reflujo (m)	reflux
refrigerio (m)	snack
refuerzo (m)	booster shot
regadera (f)	shower
régimen (m)	diet
regla (f) period	menstruation, menstrual
regla menstruación (f) menses	menstrual period, menstruation,
regurgitación (f)	regurgitation
rehabilitación (f)	rehabilitation
rehabilitar (vb)	to rehabilitate
rehidratar (vb)	to rehydrate
relaciones sexuales (f/pl) intercourse/relations	sexual
relajado (adj)	relaxed

religión (f)	religion
religioso/religiosa (adj)	religious
rellenar (vb)	to refill
relleno (m)	filling
remedio (m)	cure, remedy
remedios (m/pl)	legal drugs
remedios caseros (m/pl)	home remedies
remisión (f)	remission
renquear (vb)	to limp
renunciar (vb)	to quit
repetir (vb, col)	to burp
replicar (vb)	to replicate
reproducción (f)	reproduction
reproducir (vb)	to reproduce
resaca (f)	hangover
resbalar (vb)	to slip
reseca (f)	chapped skin
resección (f)	resection
resequedad (f)	dryness
resistencia (f)	resistance
resfriado (m)	cold (illness)
resfriado común (m)	common cold
resfriado en el pecho (m)	chest cold
resfrío (m)	congestion, cold (illness)
resollar (vb)	to breathe
respiración (f)	breath
respiración artificial (f)	artificial respiration
respirador (m)	respirator
respirando con chiflidos (m)	wheezing
respirando con silbidos (m)	wheezing
respirar (vb)	to breathe
respirar con chiflidos (vb)	to wheeze
respirar con silbidos (vb)	to wheeze
respiratorio/respiratoria (adj)	respiratory
resucitación (f)	resuscitation
resucitación cardiopulmonar (f)	CPR
resucitar (vb)	to resuscitate
resultado (m)	result
retardo (m)	retardation
retención (f)	retention
retina (f)	retina
retinitis (f)	retinitis
retirada (f)	withdrawal
retorcijones (m/pl)	cramps, abdominal
cramps	
retraso (m)	retardation

retraso mental (m)	mental retardation
reuma (f)	arthritis
reumatismo (m)	rheumatism
revisar (vb)	to examine
revisión de sus partes (f)	pelvic exam
revivir (vb)	to revive
riesgo (m)	risk
rigidez (f)	rigidity
rigidez abdominal (f)	abdominal rigidity
rígido/rígida (adj)	stiff, rigid
rigor mortis (m)	rigor mortis
rinitis (f)	rhinitis, stuffy nose
rinitis alérgica (f)	hay fever
riñón (m)	kidney
rinoplastia (f)	rhinoplasty
ritmo cardíaco (m)	heartbeat
roble venenoso (m)	poison oak
rodilla (f)	knee
rollo cervical (m)	cervical roll
rollo lumbar (m)	lumbar roll
romo/roma (adj)	dull
romper (vb)	to break
romper fuente (vb)	to break water
romper la bolsa de agua (vb)	to break water
roñas (f/pl)	hives
roncar (vb)	to snore
roncha (f)	welt
ronchas (f/pl)	rash, hives
ronco/ronca (adj)	hoarse
ronquera (f)	huskiness, hoarseness
ronquido (m)	snore
ropa (f)	clothing
rosácea (f)	rosacea
roséola (f)	roseola
rostro (m, col)	face
roto/rota (adj)	broken
rótula (f)	patella, kneecap
rotura de trompas (f)	tubal rupture
rotura (f)	rupture, break, hernia
rozadura (f)	chafe
rubéola (f)	rubella, German measles
rubor (m)	flush
ruptura (f)	rupture
ruptura uterine (f)	uterine rupture

sabor (m)	taste, flavor
sacaleche (m)	breast pump
sacar (vb)	to take out, remove
sacar aire (vb)	to burp
sacar sangre (vb)	to draw blood
saco amniótico (m)	amniotic sac
sacudida (f)	tic
sal (f)	salt
sala (f)	ward
sala de bebés (f)	nursery
sala de cirugía (f)	operating room
sala de cuidados intensivos (f)	intensive care
sala de emergencia (f)	emergency room
sala de espera (f)	waiting room
sala de labor y partos (f)	labor and delivery room
sala de maternidad (f)	maternity ward
sala de operaciones (f)	operating room
sala de recuperación (f)	recovery room
salida de los dientes (f)	teething
salino/salina (adj)	saline
salir sangre (vb)	to hemorrhage
salirle leche (vb)	to lactate
saliva (f)	saliva, sputum
salmonella (f)	salmonella
salpullido (m)	hives*, rash, heat rash
saltos del corazón (m/pl)	heart palpitations
salubridad (f)	health
salud (f)	health
salud mental (f)	mental health
saludable (adj)	healthy
sangrado (m)	hemorrhage, bleeding
sangrado por la nariz (m)	nosebleed
sangrado vaginal (m)	vaginal bleeding
sangrado vaginal ligero (m)	spotting
sangramiento (m)	bleeding
sangrar (vb)	to bleed, hemorrhage
sangre (f)	blood
sangre coagulada (f)	blood clot
sangre débil (f, col)	anemia
sangre en el esputo (f)	bloody sputum
sangre en el excremento (f)	bloody stool
sangre en la orina (f)	bloody urine
sangre en las heces (f)	bloody stool
sangre pobre (f, col)	anemia
sangre por la nariz (f)	bloody nose

sangría (f)	bleeding
sanguijuela (f)	leech
sanitario/sanitaria (adj)	sanitary
sano/sana (adj)	healthy, sane
sarampión (m)	measles
sarampión alemán (m)	German measles, rubella
sarampión regular (m)	measles
sarcoma (m)	sarcoma
sarna (f)	mange, scabies
sarpullido de calor (m)	heat rash
sarro (m)	plaque, tartar
satisfecho/satisfecha (adj)	satisfied
seco/seca (adj)	dry
secreción (f)	discharge, secretion
secreción de la vagina (f)	vaginal discharge
secreción de los senos (f)	breast discharge
secreción nasal (f)	runny nose
secreción por el pene (f)	penile discharge
secretar (vb)	to secrete
secundinas (f/pl)	afterbirth
sed (f)	thirst
sedado (adj)	sedated
sedante (m)	sedative
sedentario/sedentaria (adj)	sedentary
seguido/seguida (adv)	frequent
seguimiento (m)	follow-up
seguro/segura (adj)	safe
seguro (m)	insurance
seguro médico (m)	medical insurance
sellante (m)	sealant
semen (m)	semen
semilla (f)	sperm
senil (adj)	senile
senilidad (f)	senility
seno (m)	sinus, chest, breast
señor (m)	man
senos (m/pl)	sinuses
senos nasales (m/pl)	nasal sinuses
sensación (f)	sensation
sensación de ardor (f)	burning sensation
sensación de desmayo (f)	light-headedness
sensación de náuseas (f)	nauseous feelings
sensaciones de ardor (f/pl)	burning feelings
sensaciones quemantes (f/pl)	burning feelings
sensibilidad (f)	sensitivity
sensible (adj)	sensitive
sentir(se) (vb)	to feel

sentir comezón (vb)	to itch
sentir náusea(s) (vb)	to gag
sentir picazón (vb)	to itch
sequedad (f)	dryness
sequedad vaginal (f)	vaginal dryness
ser humano (m)	human being
ser internado/internada (vb)	to be admitted
sereno/serena (adj)	calm
serio/seria (adj)	serious
serología (f)	serology
serpigo (m)	ringworm
servicio (m)	bathroom
servicios de médicos (m/pl)	health care
servicios de salud (m/pl)	health care
servilleta sanitaria (f)	sanitary napkin
seso (m, col)	brain
severamente enflaquecido (adj)	emaciated
severo/severa (adj)	severe
sexo (m)	sex
sexualidad (f)	sexuality
shock anafiláctico (m)	anaphylactic shock
sibilancia (f)	wheezing
SIDA (m)	AIDS
sien (f)	temple (of the head)
siesta (f)	nap
sífilis (f)	syphilis
sigmoidoscopia (f)	sigmoidoscopy
signos vitales (m/pl)	vital signs
silba (f)	wheeze
silbarle el pecho (vb)	to wheeze
silbido (m)	whistle
silencioso/silenciosa (adj)	quiet
silla de ruedas (f)	wheelchair
silla retrete (f)	commode
sin sueño (adj)	sleepless
sin vida (adj)	lifeless
síndrome (m)	syndrome
síndrome alcohol fetal (m)	fetal alcohol syndrome
sindrome del tunel carpiano (m)	carpal tunnel syndrome
Síndrome de Down (m)	Down Syndrome
síndrome de intestino irritable (m)	irritable bowel syndrome
síndrome premenstrual – SPM (m)	premenstrual syndrome - PMS
síndrome respiratorio agudo grave (m) SARS	severe acute respiratory syndrome
singulto (m)	hiccups
sino que escupe sangre (m)	blood-spitting sinus

sintético/sintética (adj)	synthetic
síntomas (m/pl)	symptoms
sintomática (adj)	symptomatic
sinusitis (f)	sinusitis
sistema circulatorio (f)	circulatory system
sistema immune (f)	immune system
sistema nervioso (f)	nervous system
sobaco (m, col)	armpit
sobar (vb)	to massage, rub
sobredosis (f)	overdose
sobrepeso/sobrepesa (adj)	overweight
sobrevivir (vb)	to survive
sobrio/sobria (adj)	sober
socorro (m)	help
sodio (m)	sodium
sofocación (f)	suffocation
sofoco (m)	suffocation, shortness of breath
sofocones (m/pl, col)	hot flashes
solitaria (f)	tapeworm
soltura (f, col)	diarrhea
somnifero (m)	sleeping pill
somnolencia (f)	lethargy
somnoliento (adj)	drowsy, sleepy
sonda (f)	catheter, tube
sondear (vb)	to catheterize
sonido intestinal (m)	bowel sound
sonografía (f)	ultrasound
sonograma (m)	sonogram
soñoliento/soñolienta (adj)	sleepy, drowsy
soplo en el corazón (m)	heart murmur
soplo del corazón (m)	heart murmur
soportar (vb)	to support
soporte (m)	brace
sordera (f)	deafness
sordo/sorda (adj)	deaf, dull
sordo (m), sorda (f)	deaf person, deaf
sordo-mudo (adj)	deaf-mute
sordo-mudo (m/f)	deaf-mute person
soriasis (f)	psoriasis
soroche (m)	mountain sickness
sostener (vb)	to support
spray nasal (m)	spray nasal
suave (adj)	soft
subir de peso (vb)	to gain weight
subnutridos/desnutridas (adj)	undernourished
sucio/sucia (adj)	dirty

sudar (vb)	to perspire, sweat
sudor (m)	perspiration, sweat
sudores nocturnos (m/pl)	night sweats
sudores por la noche (m/pl)	night sweats
sueño (m)	dream, sleep
suero (m)	serum, I.V.
sufrir (vb)	to suffer
suicidarse (vb)	to commit suicide
suicidio (m)	suicide
sumbido en los oídos (m, col)	buzzing in the ears
suplemento (m)	supplement
suplementos de hierro (m/pl)	iron supplements
supositorio (m)	suppository
supuración (f)	pus
supurar (vb)	to drain
surtido nuevo (m)	refill
surtir (vb)	to refill
susceptible (adj)	susceptible
susto (m)	fear, fright, folk illness
sutura (f)	suture
suturar (vb)	to stitch, suture

T

tabaco (m)	tobacco
tabique (m)	septum, nasal septum
tableta (f)	tablet
tablilla (f)	splint
TAC (m)	CAT scan
tachas (f/p)	blemishes
tacotillo (m)	skin boil
tacto (m)	touch
tacto rectal (m)	rectal exam
tajo (m)	gash
talco (m)	talcum powder
talle (m, col)	waist
talón (m)	heel
tampón (m)	tampon
tapones para los oídos (m/pl)	earplugs
taquicardia (f)	arrhythmia
starjeta de seguro médico (f)	insurance card
tartamudear (vb)	to stutter
tartamudeo (m)	stuttering, stammering
tartamudez (f)	stuttering, stammering
tatuaje (m)	tattoo

técnico(m)/técnica (f)	technician
técnico de radiografía (m)	x-ray technician
técnica de radiografía (f)	x-ray technician
tejido (m)	tissue
tejido graso (m)	fatty tissue
tejido muscular (m)	muscle tissue
temblores (m/pl)	tremors, shakes
temperatura (f)	fever, temperature
temperatura normal (f)	basic body temperature (BBT)
temporal (adj)	temporary
tenazas (f/pl)	forceps
tendón (m)	tendon
tendón de la corva (m)	hamstring
tendinitis (f)	tendonitis
tener angustia (vv)	to be anxious
tener ansias (vb)	to be anxious
tener basca (vb)	to throw up
tener chillidos (vb)	to wheeze
tener coraje (vb)	to be depressed
tener el susto (vb)	to be depressed
tener la congestión (vb)	to be congested
tener sangramiento (vb)	hemorrhage
tener sed (vb)	to be thirsty
tener sueño (vb)	to be sleepy
tener tapados (vb)	to be congested
tener tristeza (vb)	to be sad, to be depressed
tener vómitos (vb)	to be vomiting
tenia (f)	tapeworm
tensión (f)	strain
tensión alta (f)	hypertension
tensión emocional (f)	stress
tensión nerviosa (f)	nervous strain
terapeuta (m/f)	therapist
terapeuta del habla (m/f)	speech therapist
terapeuta del lenguaje (m/f)	speech therapist
terapeuta físico (m/f)	physical therapist
terapeuta ocupacional (m/f)	occupational therapist
terapia (f)	therapy
terapia física (f)	physical therapy - PT
terminal (adj)	terminal
terminar (vb)	to finish
termómetro (m)	thermometer
terror (m)	fright
testamento en vida (m)	advance health care directive
testículos (m/pl)	testicles
testosterona (f)	testosterone
tétano (m)	tetanus

tete (m)	pacifier
tetera (f)	nipple (of nursing bottle)
tetilla (f)	nipple (of a male)
tez (f)	complexion
tibio/tibia (adj)	lukewarm
tic (m)	tic
tiempo (m)	weather, time
tiezo/tieza (adj)	stiff
tifus (m)	typhus
tijeras (f/pl)	scissors
tímpano (m)	eardrum
tímpano roto (m)	eardrum perforation
tiña (f)	ringworm
tiña inguinal (f)	jock itch
tinitus (m)	tinnitus, buzzing in the ears
tintineo (m)	ringing/buzzing in the ears
tintura (f)	tincture
tira de prueba (f)	test strip
tiraleche (m)	breast pump
tirisia (f, col)	jaundice
tirita (f)	bandage
tiritar (vb)	to shiver
tiritones (m/pl)	tremors, convulsions
tiroides (f)	thyroid gland, thyroid
tirón (m)	tic
tisis (f)	tuberculosis
toalla (f)	towel
toalla femenina (f)	sanitary napkin
toalla sanitaria (f)	sanitary napkin
tobillo (m)	ankle
tocar (vb)	to touch
tolerar (vb)	to tolerate
tomar (vb)	to drink, take
tomografía (f)	computerized axial tomography - CAT
tomografía computarizada (f)	computerized tomography – CT scan
tónico (adj)	tonic
tónico (m)	tonic
tono cardiaco fetal (m)	fetal heart tone
tonsilectomía (f)	tonsillectomy
tonsilitis (f)	tonsilitis
tórax (m)	thorax, chest
torcedura (f)	sprain

torcedura del tobillo (f)	ankle sprain
torcer(se) (vb)	to sprain
torcido/torcida (adj)	twisted
torcijones (m/pl)	abdominal cramps
torniquete (m)	tourniquet
tortícolis (f)	stiff neck
torzoncitos (m/pl, col)	abdominal cramps
torzones (m/pl, col)	abdominal cramps
tos (f)	cough
tos ahogona (f)	pertussis
tos convulsiva (f)	pertussis, whooping cough
tos ferina (f)	pertussis, whooping cough
tos seca (f)	dry cough
toser (vb)	to cough
toxemia (f)	toxemia
tóxico/tóxica (adj)	toxic, poisonous
toxina (f)	toxin
trabajador (m)/trabajadora (f) social	social worker
trabajo de parto (m)	labor
tracción (f)	traction
tragadero (m, col)	esophagus
tragante (m, col)	esophagus
tragar (vb)	to swallow
tranquilizante (adj)	tranquilizer
tranquilizante (m)	tranquilizer
tranquilo/tranquila (adj)	calm
transfusión (f)	transfusion
transfusión de sangre (f)	blood transfusion
transitorio/transitoria (adj)	temporary
transmitido/transmitida (adj)	transmitted
transmitido sexualmente (adj)	sexually-transmitted
transpiración (f)	perspiration
transpirar (vb)	to perspire
tráquea (f)	trachea
trasplantar (vb)	to transplant
trasplante (m)	transplant
trasplante de corazón (m)	heart transplant
trasplante de cornea (m)	corneal transplant
trastornado/transtornada (adj)	upset, mentally deranged
trastornar (vb)	to upset
trastorno (m)	disorder, confusion
trastorno bipolar (m)	bipolar disorder
trastorno de deficiencia de concentración (m) (ADD)	attention deficit disorder
trastorno del equilibrio (m)	vertigo

trastorno mental (m)	mental illness/disorder
trastorno obsesivocompulsivo (m)	obsessive compulsive disorder
tratamiento (m)	treatment
tratamiento de canal (m)	root canal
tratamiento con láser (m)	laser treatment
tratamiento hormonal (m)	hormone treatment
tratamiento untravioleta (m)	ultraviolet treatment - UVA
tratamientos alternativos (m/pl)	alternative treatments
tratar (vb)	to treat
trauma (m)	trauma
traumatismo (m)	trauma
trauma en la cabeza (m)	head trauma, head injury
traumático/traumática (adj)	traumatic
trazas (f/pl)	traces
tremores (m/pl)	tremors
tríceps (m)	triceps
tricomonas (f/pl)	trichomonas
trimestre (m)	trimester
tripa (f)	bowel, intestine, gut
tripita (f, col)	appendix
trismo (m)	lockjaw
triste (adj)	sad
tristeza (f)	grief
trocitos (m/pl)	lozenges
trombosis (f)	thrombosis
trombosis coronaria (f)	coronary thrombosis
trompa (f)	tube
trompa de eustaquio (f)	eustachian tube
trompas de Falopio (f/pl)	Fallopian tubes
tuberculosis (f)	tuberculosis - TB
tubo (m)	tube
tubo de ensayo (m)	test tube
tubo Falopio (m)	Fallopian tubes
tuétano (m, col)	bone marrow
tumor (m)	tumor, melanoma, growth
tumor maligno (m)	malignant tumor
tumor nocivo (m)	carcinoma
tumorcito (m)	growth
turno (m)	appointment

U

úlcera (f)	sore, ulcer
úlcera de cama (f)	bed sore
úlcera de decúbito (f)	bed sore

úlcera del estómago (f)	stomach ulcer
úlcera gástrica (f)	gastric ulcer
úlcera péptica (f)	peptic ulcer
úlceras de la boca (f/pl)	cold sores
ultrasonido (m)	ultrasound
ultrasonografía (f)	ultrasound
unidad de cuidado intensive (f)	critical care unit – CCU
unidad the cuidado intensive (f)	intensive care unit - ICU
uña (f)	nail
uña del pie encarnada (f)	ingrown toenail
uña encarnada (f)	ingrown nail
uña enterrada (f)	ingrown nail
uncinaria (f)	hookworm
uñero (m)	hangnail
ungüento (m)	cream, ointment
uremia (f)	uremia
urétra (f)	urethra
urgencia urinaria (f)	urinary urgency
urgente (adj)	urgent
urinálisis (f)	urinalysis
urinario/urinaria (adj)	urinary
urología (f)	urology
urólogo(m), uróloga (f)	urologist
urticaria (f)	hives
usar (vb)	to use
uso de drogas (m)	drug use
útero (m)	womb, uterus
uvula (f)	uvula

V

vacín (m)	basin, bedpan
vacín de cama (m)	bedpan
vacuna (f)	immunization, vaccine
vacunación (f)	vaccination
vacunar (vb)	to immunize, vaccinate
vagina (f), vajina (f)	vagina
vaginal (adj)	vaginal
vaginitis (f)	vaginitis
válvula (f)	valve
várice (f)	varicose vein
varicela (f)	chicken pox
varices (f/pl)	varicose veins
varón (m)	male
vascular (adj)	vascular
vasectomía (f)	vasectomy

vasija (f)	basin
vaso de noche (m)	urinal
vasos sanguíneos (m/pl)	blood vessels
vegetativo/vegatativa (adj)	vegetative
vejez (f)	old age
vejiga (f)	bladder, blister
vejiga hiperactiva (f)	overactive bladder
vello (m)	body hair, fuzz
vena (f)	vein
vena varicosa (f)	varicose vein
vencimiento (f)	expiration
venda (f)	bandage
vendaje (m)	bandage, dressing
veneno (m)	venom, toxin, poison
veneno de abeja (m)	bee venom
venenoso/venenosa (adj)	poisonous
ventana nasal (f)	nostril
ventanas de la nariz (f)	nostrils
ventanilla (f)	nostril
ventilador (m)	ventilator
ventrículo (m)	ventricle
ver (vb)	to see
verdugón (m)	welt
vergüenza (f)	embarrassment
verruga (f)	wart
verrugas genitales (f/pl)	genital warts
vértebras (f/pl)	vertebrae
vértigo (m)	vertigo
vesícula (f)	gall bladder
vesícula biliar (f)	gall bladder
víctima (f)	victim
vida (f)	life
viejo (m), vieja (f)	old man/woman
viento (m)	flatulence
vientre (m)	belly, abdomen
vigilancia (f)	follow-up
VIH (m)	HIV
violación (f)	rape
violado/violada (adj)	raped
viral (adj)	viral
vírico/vírica (adj)	viral
viril (adj)	virile
viruela (f)	smallpox
viruela loca (f)	chicken pox
virus (m)	virus
virus de estómago (m)	stomach virus

virus de inmunodeficiencia humana HIV	Human Immunodeficiency Virus -
vísceras (f/pl)	gut
visión (f)	sight, vision
visión borrosa (f)	blurred vision
vision del tunel (f)	tunnel vision
visión doble (f)	double vision
visita (vb)	to visit
vista (f)	sight, eyesight, vision, eye
vista borrosa (f)	blurred vision
vista doble (f)	double vision
vista emborronada (f)	blurred vision
vista nublada (f)	blurred vision
vital (adj)	vital
vitamina (f)	vitamin
vivir (vb)	to live
vivo/viva (adj)	alive
vólvulo (m)	volvulus, bowel obstruction
vomitar (vb)	to throw up, vomit
vómito (m)	vomit
voz (f)	voice

X

xenofobia (f)	xenophobia

Y

yema (f)	finger pad
yema del dedo (f)	fingertip
yerbero(m), yerbera (f)	herbalist
yeso (m)	cast
yodo (m)	iodine
yugular (adj)	jugular

Z

zafada (f, col)	dislocation
zafar (vb)	to dislocate
zambo/zamba (adj)	bowlegged
zona (f, col)	shingles
zoster (m, col)	herpes zoster, shingles

zumaque venenoso (m)	poison sumac
zumbido en los oidos (m)	ringing/buzzing in the ears
zurdo/zurda (adj)	left-handed

English – Spanish Medical Dictionary

	A	

abdomen	el vientre, el abdomen
abdominal	abdominal
abdominal cramps	los retorcijones, los cólicos (col)
abdominal discomfort	la molestia abdominal
abdominal distention	la distensión abdominal
abdominal rigidity	la rigidez abdominal
abdominal surgery	la cirugía abdominal
abnormal	anormal
abnormality	la anormalidad
abortion	el aborto, el fracaso, el malogro
abrasion	la abrasión
abscess	el absceso, el postema
abscesses l	os furúnculos, los nacidos
absorption	la absorción
abstinance	la abstinencia
abuse	el abuso
abused	engañado/engañada
accident	el accidente
acetaminophen	el acetaminofén
ache	el dolor, la pena
acid	el ácido
acne	la acné, las espinillas, los granitos
active	enérgico/enérgica, activo
acupuncture	la acupuntura
acute pain	agudo
Adam's apple	la nuez de la garganta, la nuez de Adán
addict	el adicto/la adicta

addiction	la adicción
adhesion	la adhesion
adolescence	la adolescencia
adolescent	la/el adolescente
adopted	adoptivo/adoptiva
adoption	la adopción
adrenal glands	las glándulas adrenales
adrenaline	la adrenalina
adult	el adulto/la adulta
adverse reaction	la reacción adverse
advice	el consejo
afterbirth	el nacimiento postumo, las secundinas
age	la edad
agent	el/la agente
agitation	la agitación
AIDS	el SIDA
AIDS test	la prueba de SIDA
ailment	la dolencia, el padecimiento
air	el aire
albacore	la albacora
albino	el albino, la albina
albumin	la albúmina
alcoholic	el alcohólico, la alcohólica
alcoholism	el alcoholismo, la dipsomanía
alert	alerta
alive	vivo/viva
alkalosis	la alcalosis
allergen	el alérgeno
allergic	alérgico
allergic reactions	las reacciones alérgicas
allergist	el/la alergista
allergy	la alergia
allergy test	la prueba para alergias
alopecia	la alopecia
alternative treatments	los tratamientos alternativos
alveoli	los alvéolos
ambidextrous	ambidextro
ambulance	la ambulancia
amenorrhea	la amenorrea
amino acid	el aminoácido
ammonia	el amoníaco
amnesia	la amnesia
amniocentesis	la amniocentesis
amniotic fluid	el liquido amniótico
amniotic sac	el saco amniótico

amphetamines	las anfetaminas, las pirulas (col)
amputation	la amputación
amputee	el amputado/la amputada
analgesic	el analgésico
analysis	el análisis
anaphylactic reaction	la reacción anafiláctica
anaphylactic shock	el shock anafiláctico
anatomy	la anatomía
ancestor	el antepasado/la
antepasada	
andropause	la andropausia-climaterio
masculine	
anemia	la anemia
anemic	anémico
anesthesia	la anestesia
anesthesiologist	el anestesiólogo/la anestesióloga
aneurysm	el aneurisma
anger	el enojo
angina	la angina de pecho
angiogram	la angiograma
angioplasty	la angioplastia
ankle	el tobillo
ankle sprain	la torcedura del tobillo
anorexia	la anorexia
antacid	el antiácido
anthrax	el ántrax
antibacterial	la antibacteriano
antibiotic	el antibiótico
antibodies	los anticuerpos
anticoagulant	el anticoagulante
antidepressant	el antidepresivo
antidote	el antídoto
antihistamine	el antihistamínico
anti-inflammatory	el anti-inflamatorio
antimalarial	el antipalúdico
antiseptic	el antiseptico
anus	el ano
anxiety	la ansiedad
anxious	ansioso/ansiosa
aorta	la aorta
apathy	la apatía
apnea	la apnea
appendectomy	la apendectomía
appendicitis	la apendicitis
appendix	el apéndice, la tripita (col)
appetite	el apetito

applicator	el aplicador
appointment	la cita, el turno
arm	el brazo
armpit	la axila, el sobaco (col)
arrhythmia	la arritmia, la taquicardia
arterial occlusion	la oclusión de una arteria
artery	la arteria
arthritis	la artritis, la reuma
artificial insemination	la inseminación artificial
artificial respiration	la respiración artificial
asbestos	el asbesto
asphyxia	la asfixia
aspirin	la aspirina
asthma	el asma, el mal de pecho (col)
asthmatic	asmático/asmático
astigmatism	el astigmatismo
athlete's foot	los hongos en los pies, el
pie de atleta	
atrium	el atrio
atrophy	la atrofia
auditory canal	el conducto auditivo
autism	el autismo
autoimmune illness	la enfermedad
autoinmune	
autopsy	la autopsia
awake	despierto/despierta

B

baby	el/la bebé
baby bottle	la mamadera
baby food	la comidita de bebé
back	la espalda, el espinazo
back of neck	la nuca
back pain	el dolor de espalda
backbone	la columna vertebral, el
espinazo	
bacteria	la bacteria
bad	malo/mala
bad breath	el mal aliento
balance	el equilibrio
balanced diet	la alimentación
equilibrada	
bald	el calvo/la calva, pelado
baldness	la calvicie
bandage	el vendaje, la venda

bandaid	la curita
barbiturates	los barbitúricos
bariatric surgeon	el cirujano bariátrico
barium	el bario
basic body temperature (BBT)	la temperatura normal
basin	el vacín, la vasija
bassinet	los moisés
bath	el baño
bathroom	el servicio, el excusado
bed	la cama
bed rest	el descanso en cama
bed sore	la llaga de cama
bedbug	la chinche
bedpan	el orinal, la chata, el pato
bedridden patient	el encamado/la encamada
bed-wetting	la enuresis
bee sting	la picadura de abeja
bee venom	el veneno de abeja
behavior	la conducta
behavior patterns	los modos de conducta
belch	el eructo
belief	la creencia
belly	el vientre, la panza
belly button	el ombligo
bends	la enfermedad por descompresión
benefits	los beneficios
benign	benigno (adj)
beverage	la bebida
bib	el babero
bicuspid	el bicúspide, la premolar
biceps	el bíceps
bilirubin	la bilirrubina
bile	la bilis, la hiel
bill	la cuenta
biological	biológico
biopsy	la biopsia
bipolar disorder	el trastorno bipolar
birth	el parto, la natalidad
birth canal	el canal del parto
birth certificate	el certificado de nacimiento
birth control pill	la pastilla anticonceptiva, la pildora
birth defect	el defecto de nacimiento
birthdate	la fecha/el día de nacimiento

birthmark	la mancha de nacimiento
bite	la mordida
bitter	amargo(a)
black stool	el excremento negro
blackhead	la espinilla
bladder	la vejiga
bladder infection	la infección de vejiga
bladder stones	los cálculos en la vejiga
bleeding	la sangría, el sangrado
bleeding gums	las encías sangrantes
blemishes	los lunares, las manchas, las tachas
blepharitis	la blefaritism
blind	ciego(a)
blind person	el ciego/la ciega
blindness	la ceguera
blister	la ampolla
bloated	hinchado(a)
bloating	el gas en el estomago
blood	la sangre
blood cells	las células sanguíneas
blood clot	la sangre coagulada
blood count	el recuento globular
blood loss	la pérdida de sangre
blood platelet	la plaqueta de sangre
blood poisoning	el envenenamiento de la sangre
blood pressure	la presión arterial
blood relative	el pariente consanguineo
blood smear	la muestra de sangre
blood test	la prueba de sangre
blood thinner	el diluyente de la sangre
blood transfusion	la transfusión de sangre
blood type	el grupo sanguíneo
blood vessels	los vasos sanguíneos
blood-spitting sinus	el sino que escupe sangre
bloody nose nasal	la epistaxis, la hemorragia
bloody sputum	la sangre en el esputo
bloody stool	la sangre en las heces
bloody urine	la sangre en la orina
blurred vision	la visión borrosa
body	el cuerpo
body hair	el vello
body mass index	el índice de masa corporal
body pain	el dolor del cuerpo
bones	los huesos
bone marrow	la médula ósea

bone spur	el espolón
booster shot	la inyección de refuerzo
botulism	el botulismo
bowel	la entraña, el intestino
bowel movement	la evacuación
bowel obstruction	el vólvulo
bowel sound	el sonido intestinal
bowlegged	zambo/zamba
brain	el cerebro
brain damage	el daño cerebral
brain dead	la muerte cerebral
breast	el seno
breast discharge	la secreción de los senos
breast exam	el examen del seno
breast mass	la masa de mama
breast masses	las masas de los senos
breast milk	la leche materna
breast pump	el extractor de leche
breast self-examination	el autoexámen de mama
breastbone	el esternón
breath	la respiración, el aliento
breathing problems	los problemas respiratorios
breech delivery	el parto de nalgas
breech presentation	la presentación de nalgas
broken	fracturado/fracturada
broken bone	el hueso fracturado/quebrado
bronchial asthma	el asma bronquial
bronchitis	la bronquitis
bronchus	el bronquio
bruise	la moradura
bruised	amoratado(a)
bruised bone	el hueso magullado/golpeado
bruised muscle	el músculo magullado/golpeado
bubonic plague	la peste bubónica
bulimia	la bulimia
bulimic	bulímico(a)
bullet	el balazo
bullet wound	la herida de bala
bump	el chichón
burn	la quemadura
bunion	el juanete
burning feelings	la sensaciones de ardor
burning pain	el dolor quemante

burning sensation	la sensación de ardor
bursitis	la bursitis
buttocks	las nalgas
buzzing in the ears	el tintineo

C

caffeine	la cafeína
calf (of the leg)	la pantorrilla
callous	el callo
calorie	la caloría
calm	sereno/tranquilo, serena/tranquila
cancer	el cáncer
cancerous	canceroso(a)
canine tooth	el canino
canker sore	la postemilla
capsule	la cápsula
carcinogenic	carcinogénico(a)
carcinoma	el carcinoma, el tumor nocivo
cardiac arrest	el fallo cardíaco,, el paro cardiac
cardiac muscle	el músculo cardíaco
cardiology	la cardiología
cardiologist	el cardiólogo/la cardióloga
cardiopulmonary resuscitation - CPR	la reanimación cardiopulmonar
cardiovascular disease	la enfermedad cardiovascular
care	la asistencia
carpal tunnel syndrome	el sindrome del tunel carpiano
castration	la castración
CAT scan	el TAC
catatonic	catatónico(a)
cataract	la catarata
catheter	el catéter
cause	la causa
cavity	la picadura
cells	las células, los glóbulos
centigrade	los grados centígrados
cerebral hemorrhage	el derrame cerebral
cerebral ischemia	la isquemia cerebral
cerebral palsy	la parálisis cerebral
cervical pregnancy	el embarazo cervical
cervical roll	el rollo cervical
cervix	la cérvix, el cuello uterino
cesarean section	la operación cesárea

chafe	la rozadura
chamomile	la manzanilla
chapped skin	la piel agrietada/rajada/reseca
chart	el gráfico, la hoja clínica
checkup	el chequeo
cheeks	las mejillas
chemical	químico(a)
chemotherapy	la quimoterapia
chest	el seno/pecho, el tórax
chest discomfort	las molestias en el pecho
chest pain	el dolor de pecho
chest tightness	la presión en el pecho
chest x-ray	la radiografía del tórax
chicken pox	la viruela loca
child delivery	el parto
childhood	la infancia
chill	el resfriado, el escalofrío
chin	el mentón
chlamydia	la clamidia
choking	el episodio de atragantamiento
cholecystitis	la colecistitis
cholesterol	el colesterol
cholera	el cólera
chronic illness	la enfermedad crónica
chronic pain	el dolor crónico
cigarette	el cigarrillo
circulatory system	la sistema circulatorio
cirrhosis	la cirrosis
circumcision	la circuncisión
claustrophobia	la claustrofobia
clot	el coágulo, la embolia
cloudy urine	la orina opaca
clubfoot	el chueco, el patizambo
cocaine	la cocaína
coccygectomy	la coccigectomía
coccyx	el coxis
cochlea	la cóclea
codeine	la codeína
cogitation	la reflexión
coitus	el coito
cold	frío/fría
cold hands	las manos frías/húmedas
cold sores	las úlceras de la boca
colic	el cólico
coliphage	la colífagos

collagen	el colágeno
collapse	la caída rápida, el colapso
colon	el colon
color blindness	el daltonismo
colostrum	el calostro, el colostro
coma	el coma
comatose	comatoso(m)/comatosa(f)
commode	la silla retrete
common cold	el resfriado común
complaint	la dolencia
complete blood count - CBC	el recuento sanguíneo complete
complexion	la tez
complications	las complicaciónes
compound fracture	la fractura compuesta
computerized axial tomography - CAT	la tomografía
computerized tomography – CT scan	la tomografía computarizada
conception	la concepción
concussion	la concusión
condition	la afección/enfermedad
confidential	confidencial, secreto
confused	confundido(a)
congenital	congénito(a)
congenital defect	el defecto congénito
congested	congestionado(a)
congestion	la congestión
conjunctivitis	la conjuntivitis
consciousness	la conciencia
consent	el consentimiento
constipated	constipado(a)
constipation	el estreñimiento
consultation	la consulta
consumption	el marasmo
contact lens	el lente de contacto
contagious	contagioso(a)
contaminated	contaminado(a)
contraceptive	el anticonceptivo
contraction	la contracción
contrast material	el material de contraste
contusion	la compresión, la
contusión	
convulsions	las convulsiones
corneal transplant	el trasplante de cornea
coronary	coronario(a)
coronary heart disease	la enfermedad cardiaca coronaria
coronary thrombosis	la trombosis coronaria
corpse	el muerto/la muerta
cortisone	la cortisona

cosmetic surgery	la cirugía cosmética
cotton swab	el hisopo
cough	la tos
cough syrup	el jarabe para la tos
cramps	los retorcijones, los calambres
cranium	el cráneo
crib	la cuna, la camita
crippled	cojo(a), lisiado(a)
crippled person	el cojo/la coja, el lisiado/la lisiada
critical	critic(a)
critical care unit – CCU	la unidad de cuidado intensive
crossed eyes	los ojos bizcos
cross-eyed	bizco(a)
croup	el crup, el garrotillo
crown	la coronilla
crown (dental)	la corona
crushing pain	el dolor aplastante
crust	la escara
crutches	las muletas
cryosurgery	la criocirugía
cure	el remedio
cured	curado(a)
cut	el corte
cuticle	la cutícula
cyanosis	la cianosis
cyst	el quiste
cystitis	la cistitis
cytology	la citología

D

---

daily	cada día, diariamente
daily dose	la dosis diaria
damage	el daño
dandruff	la caspa
dangerous	peligroso(a)
day care	la guardería
day-care center	la guardería infantil
daze	el mareo
dazed	aturdido(a)
dead	muerto(a)
dead person	el muerto/la muerta
deaf	sordo(a)
deaf person	el sordo/la sorda
deaf-mute	sordomudo(a)

death	la muerte/la defunción
decayed	cariado(a), picado(a)
deceased	difunto(a), fallecido(a)
decongestant	el descongestionante
defibrillation	la desfibrilación
deformed	deformado(a)
dehydration	la deshidratación
delirium	el delirio
deltoids	los deltoides
delusion	el delirio
dementia	la demencia
dental braces	los frenillos, los frenos
dental cavities	las caries, los dientes podridos
dental filling	el empaste
dental floss	el hilo dental
dental hygientist	el/la higienista dental
dental surgery	la cirugía dental
dentist	el/la dentista
dentist's drill	la fresa
dentistry	la odontología
dentures	las dentaduras
depression	la depresión
dermatologist	el dermatólogo/la dermatóloga
desperate	desesperado
detached retina	el desprendimiento de la retina
detoxification	la detoxificación
development	el desarollo
diabetes	la diabetes
diabetic person	el diabetico/la diabética
diagnosed	diagnosticado/diagnosticada
diagnosis	la diagnosis
dialysis	la diálisis
diaper rash	la pañalitis
diarrhea	la diarrea, la colitis
diet	la dieta
digestion	la digestión
dilatation & curettage – D&C	la dilatación y curetaje
dilated	dilatado(a)
dilation	la dilatación
diphtheria	la difteria
disability	la discapacidad
disabled	inválido(a)
disabled person	el inválido/la inválida
disease	la enfermedad
discomfort	la incomodidad
disinfectant	el desinfectante

disorder	el desorden, el trastorno
distressed	angustiado(a)
diuretic	diurético
dizziness	el mareo
dizzy	mareado(a)
doctor	el doctor/medico, la
doctora/médica	
dog bite	la mordida de perro
donated	donado(a)
donor	el/la donante
dosage	la dosificación/dosis
double pneumonia	la neumonía doble
double vision	la vista/vision doble
douche	la ducha, el lavado de vagina
Down Syndrome	el Síndrome de Down
DPT (diphtheria, pertussis, tetanus)	la DPT (difteria, pertusis, tétano)
drape	la cortina
dream	el sueño
dressing	el vendaje
drooling	el enfermo de babea
dropper	el cuentagotas
drops	las gotas
drowsiness	la modorra
drowsy	soñoliento/soñolienta,
somnoliento	
drug addict	el drogadicto/la
drogadicta	
drug addiction	la drogadicción
drug use	el uso de drogas
drunk	borracho(a)
dry	seco(a)
dry cough	la tos seca
dryness	la resequedad, lo seco
dull	romo/roma
dust	el polvo
dust allergies	las reacciones alérgicas al
polvo	
dust mite	los ácaros del polvo
dwarfism	el enanismo
dyslexia	la dislexia
dysentery	la disentería
dysmenorrhea	la dismenorrea
dystrophy	la distrofia
dysuria	la disuria

ear canal	el conducto auditivo
externo	
ear drops	las gotas para el oído
ear infection	la infección de los oídos
ear wax	el cerumen
ear, nose, and throat (ENT)	oído, nariz, y garganta
earache	el dolor de oído
eardrum	el tímpano
eardrum perforation	el perforación del tímpano
earlobe	el lóbulo de la oreja
earplugs	los tapones para los oídos
eating plan	el plan de alimentación
echocardiogram	el ecocardiograma
eclampsia	la eclampsia
ectopic pregnancy	el embarazo ectópico
egg	el óvulo
ejaculation	la eyaculación
elderly	anciano(a)
elective surgery	la cirugía electiva
electrocardiogram – EKG/ECG	el electrocardiograma
electroencephalogram - EEG	el electroencefalogramo
electromyogram - EMG	el electromiograma
emaciated	demacrado(a)
emaciation	el enflaquecimiento
embryo	el embrión
embolism	la embolia
emergency room	la sala de emergencia
emphysema	la enficema
encephalitis	la encefalitis
endemic	endémico(a)
endemic illness	la enfermedad endémica
endocarditis	la endocarditis
endocrine	endocrino(a)
endocrinology	la endocrinología
endometriosis	la endometriosis
endometrium	el endometrio
endoscopy	la endoscopía
enema	el enema, la lavativa
engorged	lleno de sangre
environment	el ambiente
enzyme	la enzima
epidemic	la epidemia,
epidémico/epidémica	
epidemic illness	la enfermedad epidémica
epidural analgesia	la analgesia epidural

epiglottis	la epiglotis
episiotomy	la episiotomía
epilepsy	la epilepsia
erectile dysfunction	la disfunción erectile
erection	la erección
erosion	la erosión
estrogen	el estrógeno
ether	el éter
euthanasia	la eutanasia
examination	la examinación, el examen
exercise	el ejercicio
excrement	el excremento
exertion	el esfuerzo
exfoliation	la exfoliación
expectorant	el expectorante
expert	el experto/la experta
expiration	la vencimiento
exploratory operation	la operación exploratoria
exposure	el exposición
external	externo(a)
eye	el ojo
eye chart	la carta para agudeza
visual	
eye drops	las gotas para los ojos
eye glasses	los espejuelos
eye strain	los ojos
cansados/fatigados	
eyebrow	la ceja
eyeglasses	las gafas
eyesight	la vista

F

face	la cara
face down	boca abajo
face paleness	las palidéz de la cara
face up	boca arriba
facelift	la estética
facial paralysis	la parálisis facial
facial skin	el cuero (col), el pellojo
(col)	
fahrenheit	fahrenheit
faint	débil
fainting spells	los desfallecimientos, los
desmayos	

fall	la caída
fallen fontanelle	la mollera caída
Fallopian tubes	las trompas de Falopio
false teeth	los dientes postizos
family	la familia
family planning	la planificación familiar
farsighted	hipermétrope
fat	gordo/gorda
fat (in food)	la grasa
fat person	el gordo/la gorda
fatal	fatal
fat-free	descremado/descremada
fatigue	la fatiga
fatty tissue	el tejido graso
fear	el miedo, el susto
fecal incontinence	la incontinencia de heces
feces	las fecales, las heces
female	la hembra
female sterility	la esterelidad femenina
femur	el fémur
fertile	fértil
fertilization	la fecundación, la fertilización
fetal alcohol syndrome	el síndrome alcohol fetal
fetal heart tone	el tono cardiaco fetal
fetal monitor	el monitoreo fetal
fetus	el feto
fever	la fiebre
fever blister	la ampolla de fiebre
fiber	la fibra
fibrillation	la fibrilación
fibroid	el fibroideo, el fibroide
fibula	el peroné
fight	la lucha, la pelea
file	el expediente
filling	el relleno
finger	el dedo
fingertip	la yema del dedo
fire	el fuego
firefighter	el bombero/la bombera
first aid	los primeros auxilios
fissure	la fisura
fist	el puño
flake	la escama
flank pain	el dolor del costado
flat foot	el pie plano
flatulance	la flatulencia

flavor	el sabor
flea	la pulga
flexible	flexible
floater (of the eye)	la estrellita
floaters	los flotadores
flu	la monga
fluoride	el fluoruro
fluoroscopy	la fluoroscopia
flush	el rubor
flushed	colorado/colorada
flutter	flúter
fly agaric	los hongos venenosos
foam	la espuma
folic acid	el ácido fólico
folk healer	el curandero/la curandera
folk healing	el curanderismo
follicle	el folículo
follicle stimulating hormone (FSH)	hormona estimulante para el folículo
follow-up	el examen de seguimiento
fontanelle	la fontanela, la mollera
food	la comida
food allergy	la alergia a los alimentos
foot	el pie
forceps	los fórceps, las pinzas
forearm	el antebrazo
forehead	la frente
foreskin	el prepucio
form	el formulario
formula	la fórmula
foster child	el hijo/la hija de crianza
fracture	la fractura
freckle	la peca
frequency	la frecuencia
frequent	seguido/seguida
fright	el susto
frigidity	la frigidez
frostbite	el congelado/el congelamiento
frozen shoulder	el hombro congelado
fumes	el humo
fungal infection	la infección por hongos, los jiotes
fungus	el hongo

gall bladder	la vesícula biliar
gall bladder disease	la enfermedad de la vesícula
gallstones	los cálculos en la vesícula
gangrene	la gangrena
gas	el gas, el flato
gash	la cuchillada, la tajo
gasping	el jadeo
gastric juice	el jugo gástrico
gastric ulcer	la úlcera gástrica
gastritis	la gastritis
gastroenterologist	el gastroenterólogo/la gastroenteróloga
gastroenterology (GI)	la gastroenterología
gastrointestinal (GI)	gastrointestinal
gauze	la gasa
gel	el gel
gender	el género
general malaise	el malestar general
generic drugs	los medicamentos genericos
genes	los genes
genetic	genético/genética
genital warts	las verrugas genitales
genitalia	las partes genitales
geriatric	geriátrico/geriátrica
geriatrics	el geriatria
germ	el germen
German measles	la rubéola
gestation	la gestación
gestational diabetes	la diabetes gestacional
giantism	el gigantismo
giardia	la giardia
gigantism	el gigantismo
gingivitis	la gingivitis
gland	la glándula
glasses	los lentes
glaucoma	la glaucoma
glove	el guante
glucose	la glucosa
glucose tests	las pruebas de glucosa
gluten	el gluten
glyburide	la gliburida
glycosuria	el glicusoria
goiter	el bocio
golfer's elbow	el codo de golfista

gonorrhea	la gonorrea
goose bumps	la piel de gallina
gout	la gota, la podagra
gown	la bata
graft	el injerto
gram	el gramo
Graves Disease	la enfermedad de Graves
grief	la pena, la tristeza, el pesar
groin	la ingle
growth	el crecimiento, el tumorcito
guilt	la culpa
gums	las encías
gun	el fusil, la pistola
gut	las vísceras
gynecologist	el ginecólogo/la ginecóloga
gynecology	la ginecología

H

habit	el hábito, la costumbre
habit-forming	que crea hábito
hair	las greñas, el pelo
hairline fracture	la fisura
halitosis	el halitosis, el mal aliento
hallucination	la halucinación
hamstring	el tendón de la corva
hand	la mano
handicap	el impedimento, la incapacidad
handicapped	el discapacitado/la discapacitada
hangnail	el uñero, el padrastro
hangover	la cruda, la goma, la resaca
happy	dichoso/dichosa, feliz
hardening	el endurecimiento
harmful	dañino/dañina
harmless	inofensivo/inofensiva
hay fever	la fiebre del heno
head	la cabeza
head injury	el golpe en la cabeza
head lice	los piojos de la cabeza
head trauma	el golpe en la cabeza

headache	el dolor de cabeza
health	la salud
health care	los servicios de salud
healthy	sano/sana, saludable
hearing	la audición
hearing aids	los audífonos
hearing test	el examen de la audición
heart	el corazón
heart attack	el ataque cardíaco
heart disease	la enfermedad del corazón
heart failure	la insuficiencia cardíaca
heart murmur	el soplo en el corazón
heart palpitations	los saltos del corazón
heart transplant	el trasplante de corazón
heartbeat	el latido del corazón
heartburn	la acidez estomacal
heat rash	el salpullido
heat stroke	el golpe de calor
heating pad	la almohadilla eléctrica
heel	el talón
height	la altura
help	la asistencia, la ayuda, el socorro
hematoma	el hematoma
hemoglobin	la hemoglobina
hemophilia	la hemofilia
hemorrhage	la hemorragia
hemorrhoids	los hemorroides
hepatitis	la hepatitis
hepatitis A/B/C	la hepatitis tipo A/B/C
herb	la hierba
herbalist	el yerbero/la yerbera
hereditary	hereditario/hereditaria
heredity	la herencia
hermaphrodite	el/la hermafrodita
hernia	la hernia, la rotura
heroin	la heroína
herpes	el herpes, la infección vírica
heterosexual	el/la heterosexual
hiccups	el hipo
high blood pressure	la presión alta
high cholesterol	el colesterol alto
hip	la cadera
hives	las ronchas
hoarse	ronco/ronca
hoarseness	la ronquera

home remedies	los remedios caseros
homeopathy	la homeopatía
homesickness	la nostalgia del hogar
homosexual	el/la homosexual
hookworm	la anquilostomosis
hopeless	desesperado
hormonal	hormonal
hormone	la hormona
hormone treatment	el tratamiento hormonal
hospital	el hospital
hot and cold spells	los periodos de calor y frio
hot flashes	los sofocos
hot pack	la compresa caliente
household chemicals	los químicos para el hoga
human	humano, el human
human bite	la mordedura humana
Human Immunodeficiency Virus - HIV	el virus de inmunodeficiencia humana
hunchback	el jorobado/la jorobada
hunger	el hambre
hungry	hambre
hurt	lastimado/lastimada
huskiness	la ronquera
hydrogen peroxide	el peróxido de hidrógeno
hygiene	el aseo, la higiene
hymen	el himen
hyperacidity	la hiperacidez
hyperactive	hiperactivo/hiperactiva
hyperglycemia	la hiperglucemia
hypernatremia	la hipernatremia
hyperopic	el hiperópico
hypersensitivity	la hipersensibilidad
hypertension	la presión alta
hyperthermia	la hipertermia
hyperthyroidism	el hipertiroidismo
hyperventilation	la hiperventilación
hypochondria	la hipocondria
hypoglycemia	la hipoglucemia
hyponatremia	la hiponatremia
hypothalamus	el hipotálamo
hypothermia	la hipotermia
hypothyroidism	el hipotiroidismo
hypoxia	la hipoxia
hysterectomy	la histerectomía
hysteria	la histeria

I

I.V.	por vena
ibuprofen	el ibuprofén
ice	el hielo
ill	enfermo/enferma
illegal drugs	las drogas ilegales
illness	la enfermedad
immature	inmaduro/immadura
immobile	inmóvil
immobilization	la inmovilización
immune	inmune
immune system	el sistema inmunológico
immunity	la inmunidad
immunization	la inmunización, la vacuna
immunoglobulin	la inmoglubina
impacted tooth	el diente impactado
impaction	la impactación
impaired	dañado/dañada
impetigo	el impétigo
implant	el implante
implantation	la implantación
impotence	la impotencia
impregnation	la impregnación
incest	el incesto
incision	la incisión
incisor	el incisivo
incontinence	la incontinencia
incubation period	el periodo de incubación
incubator	la incubadora
incurable	incurable
indigestion	el empacho
indigestion	la indigestión
induced abortion	el aborto inducido
induced labor	el parto inducido
infancy	la infancia
infant	el/la bebé
infant	el infante
infantile paralysis	la parálisis infantil
infected	infectado/infectada
infection	la infección
infertile	estéril
infertility	la infertilidad
inflamed	inflamado/inflamada
inflammation	la inflamación
influenza	la gripe, la influenza

ingrown nail	la uña encarnada
ingrown toenail	la uña del pie encarnada
inhaler	el inhalador
injection	la inyección
injured	herido/herida, lesionado/lesionada
injury	el daño, la lastimadura
inner ear	el oído
inoculation	la inoculación
inpatient	paciente hospitalizado/hospitalizada
insane	demente, loco/loca
insanity	la demencia, la locura
insect	el insecto
insect sting	la picadura de insecto
insecticide	el insecticida
insemination	la inseminación
insomnia	el insomnio
instrument	el instrumento
insufficiency	la insuficiencia
insulin	la insulina
insurance	el seguro
insurance card	la starjeta de seguro médico
insurance company	la compañía de seguro
intensive care	la sala de cuidados intensivos
intensive care unit - ICU	la unidad de cuidados intensivos
intermittent pain	el dolor intermitente
internal	internal, interno
internist	el/la internista
interpreter	el/la intérprete
interstitial	intersticial
intestinal worm	la lombriz intestinal
intestine	el intestino
intoxicated	intoxicado/intoxicada
intoxication	la intoxicación
intrauterine device - IUD (DIU)	el dispositivo intrauterino
intravenous (I.V.)	intravenoso/intravenosa
intravenous anesthesia	la anestesia intravenosa
intravenous fluids	los líquidos intravenosos
intubation	la intubación
invalid	inválido/inválida
inverted nipple	el pezón invertido
in-vitro fertilization	la fertilización en vitro
iodine	el yodo
ipecac	la ipecacuana

iron	el hierro
iron supplements	los suplementos de hierro
irregular heartbeat	los latidos cardíacos irregulares
irregular pulse	el pulso irregular
irritable bowel syndrome	el síndrome de intestino irritable
irritation	la irritación
itch	la comezón, la picazón

J

jaundice	la ictericia
jaundice pancreatitis	la pancreatitis ictericia
jaw	la mandíbula
jelly	la jalea
jock itch	la tiña inguinal
joint pain	el dolor de las articulaciones
joints	las articulaciones
jugular	yugular
juice	el jugo

K

kidney	el riñón
kidney disease	la enfermedad del riñón
kidney failure	la insuficiencia renal
kidney infection	la infección de los riñones
kidney stones	los cálculos en el riñón
kiss	el beso
kleptomania	la cleptomanía
knee	la rodilla
kneecap	la rótula
knife	el cuchillo
knot	el nudo
knuckle	el nudillo

L

Labor	el trabajo de parto
labor and delivery room	la sala de labor y partos
labor pains	los dolores de parto

laboratory	el laboratorio
labyrinthitis	la laberintitis
laceration	la laceración
lack of appetite	el desgano
lactation	la lactancia
lactose	la lactosa
lactose intolerance	la intolerancia a la lactosa
Lamaze Method	el método de Lamaze
lame	cojo/coja
lame extremity	la extremidad lisiada/tullida
laparoscopy	la laparascopía
large intestine	el intestino grueso
laryngitis	la laringitis
larynx	la laringe
laser surgery	la cirugía laser
laser treatment	el tratamiento con láser
latex	el látex
laughing gas	el gas hilarante
laxative	el laxante, el purgante
lazy eye	el ojo perezoso
lead	el plomo
lead apron	delantal de plomo
leakage	el goteo
leech	la sanguijuela
left	izquierda
left-handed	zurdo/zurda
leg	la pierna
leg cramps	los calambres en las piernas
leprosy	la lepra
lesbian	la lesbiana
lesion	la lesión
lethargy	el letargo
leukemia	la leucemia
libido	la libido, el deseo sexual
lice	los piojos
life	la vida
life expectancy	la espectativa de vida
lifeless	sin vida
lifestyle	el estilo de vida
ligament	el ligamento
light	la luz
light-headedness	el mareo
limb	la extremidad
limp	lisiado/lisiada
liniment	el linimento

liposuction	la liposucción
lips	los labios
liquid	líquido
lisp	el ceceo
listlessness	la languidez
liver	el hígado
lobe	el lóbulo
lobotomy	la lobotomía
lockjaw	el trismo
lotion	la loción
low blood pressure	la presión baja
low calorie	baja en calorias
lower back	la espalda baja
lozenges	los trocitos
lubricant	el lubricante
lukewarm	tibio/tibia
lumbar roll	el rollo lumbar
lump	el bulto
lumpectomy	la lumpectomía
lung	el pulmon
lung disease	la enfermedad de los pulmones
lupus	el lupus
lymph	la linfa
lymph node	el ganglio linfático
lymphoma	el linfoma
Lysergic acid diethylamide - LSD	la dietilamida del ácido lisérgico

M

Magnetic Resonance Imaging - MRI	la imagen por resonancia magnética
malabsorption	la malabsorción
malaise	el malestar
malaria	el paludismo
male	el varón, masculino
malformation	la malformación
malignant	maligno/maligna
malignant tumor	el tumor maligno
malnutrition	la malnutrición
malpractice	la negligencia médica
mammogram	la mamografía
man	el hombre
mange	la sarna
mania	la manía

maniac	el maniáco/la maniáca
manic	maníaco/maníaca
manic-depressive	maníaco-
depresivo/depresiva	
marijuana	la marijuana
marital status	el estado civil
mask	la máscara
mass	la masa
massage	el masaje
mastectomy	la mastectomía
maternal	materno/materna
maternity ward	la sala de maternidad
maturity	la madurez
measles	el sarampión
medical history	la historia clínica
medical insurance	el seguro médico
medical prescription	la receta médica
medical record	el expediente médico
medication	el medicamento
medicine	el medicamento, la
medicina	
melanoma	el melanoma
melena	la melena
membrane	la membrane
memory	la memoria
meningitis	la meningitis
menopause	la menopausia
menstrual cramps	los cólicos menstruales
menstrual cycle	el ciclo menstrual
menstrual pain	el dolor menstrual
menstrual period	el período menstrual
menstruation	la menstruación
mental health	la salud mental
mental hospital	el manicomio
mental illness	el trastorno mental
mental retardation	el retraso mental
mentally deranged	trastornado/transtornada
metabolism	el metabolismo
metastasis	la metástasis del cáncer
methadone	la metadona
methamphetamine	la metanfetamina
microorganism	el microorganismo
microscope	el microscopio
microsurgery	la microcirugía
middle ear	el oído medio

middle ear infection	la infección del oído
medio	
midwife	la partera, la comadrona
migraine	la jaqueca
mildew	el mojo
milk of magnesia	la leche de magnesia
mind	la mente
mineral	el mineral
miscarriage	el aborto natural, el
malparto	
mite	el ácaro, la mota
molar	el molar
mold	el mojo
mole	el lunar
monitor	el monitor
mononucleosis	la mononucleosis
mood swing	el cambio de humor
morgue	la morgue
morning sickness	los malestares de la
mañana	
morphine	la morfina
mortality	la mortalidad
mosquito	el mosquito
mountain sickness	el soroche
mouth	la boca
mouthpiece	el protector bucal
mouthwash	el enjuague bucal
movement	el movimiento
mucous	mucoso/mucosa
mucous stool	las heces mucosas
mucus	el moco
multiple fracture	la fractura múltiple
multiple sclerosis	la esclerosis múltiple
mumps	las paperas
muscle	el músculo
muscle pain	el dolor de músculos
muscle pull	la lastimadura
muscle spasm	el espasmo muscular
muscle tear	el desgarro muscular
muscle tissue	el tejido muscular
muscle weakness	la debilidad de los
músculos	
muscular cramps	los calambres musculares
muscular dystrophy	la distrofia muscular
mushroom	el hongo
mutation	la mutación
mute	mudo/muda

mute person	el mudo/la muda
myocardia infarction	el infarto del corazón
myopia	la miopía

N

nail	la uña
naked	desnudo/desnuda
name	el nombre
nap	la siesta
nape	la nuca
narcolepsy	la narcolepsia
narcotic	el narcótico
nasal cavity	la fosa nasal
nasal discharge	la secreción nasal
nasal irrigation	la irrigación nasal
nasal septum	el tabique
nasal sinuses	los senos nasales
natural	natural
natural childbirth	el parto natural
nausea	la náusea
nauseating	
nauseabundo/nauseabunda	
navel	el ombligo
nearsightedness	la miopía
nebulizer	el nebulizador
neck	el cuello
neck brace	el collar
need	la necesidad
needle	la aguja
neonatal	neonatal
neonatal intensive care	el cuidado intensivo neonatal
nephritis	la nefritis
nerve	el nervio
nervous	nervioso/nerviosa
nervous breakdown	la crisis nerviosa
nervous disorder	el desorden nervioso
nervous system	la sistema nervioso
neuralgia	la neuralgia
neurasthenia	la neurasthenia
neuritis	la neuritis
neurologist	el neurólogo/la neuróloga
neurology	la neurología
neurosis	la neurosis
neurosurgeon	el neurocirujano/la neurocirujana

neurotic	neurótico/neurótica
neurotic person	el neurotico/la neurótica
newborn	el/la recién nacido/nacida
nicotine	la nicotina
night sweats	los sudores nocturnos
nightmare	la pesadilla
nipple	el pezón
nipple (of a male)	la tetilla
nipple (of nursing bottle)	la tetera
nitroglycerine	la nitroglicerina
node	el nodo, el nódulo
normal	normal
nose	la nariz
nosebleed	la hemorragia nasal
nostril	la fosa nasal
nourishment	la nutrición
novocaine	la novocaína
numb	entumecido/entumecida
numbness	el adormecimiento
nurse	el enfermero/la enfermera
nursery	la guardería sala, la sala de bebés
nurse's aide	el/la ayudante de enfermero
nutrient	el nutricio
nutrition	el nutrición
nutritionist	el nutriólogo/la nutrióloga

O

obese	obeso/obesa
obese person	el obeso/la obesa
obesity	la obesidad
observation	la observación
obsession	la obsesión
obsessive compulsive disorder	el trastorno obsesivocompulsivo
obstetrician	el/la obstetra
obstetrics	la obstetricia
Obstetrics/Gynecology – OB/GYN	la obstetricia y ginecología
obstruction	la obstrucción
occlusion	la oclusión
occupational therapist	el/la terapeuta ocupacional
odor	el olor
office	la oficina
oily face	la cara aceitosa

oily hair	el pelo aceitoso
oily skin	la piel aceitosa
ointment	el ungüento
old age	la vejez
old man/woman	el viejo/la vieja
oncologist	el oncólogo/la oncóloga
oncology	la oncología
onset	el inicio
ooze	el cieno
operating room	la sala de cirugía
operating table	la mesa de operaciones
operation	la operación
ophtalmology	la oftalmología
ophthalmologist	el oftalmólogo/la oftalmóloga
opium	el opio
optic	óptico/óptica
optician	el óptico/la óptica
optometrist	el/la optometrista
oral	oral
organ	el órgano
orgasm	el orgasmo
orifice	el orificio
orphan	el huérfano/la huérfana
orthodontics	la ortodoncia
orthodontist	el/la ortodoncista
orthopedic surgeon	el cirujano/la cirujana ortopédico
orthopedic surgery	la cirugía ortopédica
orthostatic blood pressure	la presión ortostática
osteoarthritis	la osteoartritis
osteopath	el/la osteópata
osteoporosis	la osteoporisis
otitis	la otitis
otolaryngologist	el otorrinolaringólogo
outer ear	la oreja
outpatient	el/la paciente externo/externa
ovarian cyst	el quiste de ovario
ovarian pain	el dolor en los ovarios
ovarian pregnancy	el embarazo ovárico
ovary	el ovario
overactive bladder	la vejiga hiperactiva
overdose	la sobredosis
over–the-counter medication – OTC	los medicamentos de venta libre
overweight	sobrepeso/sobrepesa

ovulation	la ovulación
oxygen	el oxígeno
oxygen mask	la careta de oxígeno

P

pacemaker	el marcapaso
pacifier	el chupete
pain	el dolor
pain reliever	el calmante para el dolor
painful	doloroso/dolorosa
painkiller	la pastilla para el dolor
palate	el paladar
pale	pálido/pálida
paleness	la palidez
palm	la palma
palpitations	las palpitacíones
palsy	la parálisis
pancreas	el páncreas
panic attack	el ataque de pánico
panting	el jadeo
Pap smear	el examen de Papanicolao
paralysis	la parálisis
paralyzed	paralítico/paralítica
paramedic	el paramédico/la paramédica
paranoia	la paranoia
paranoid	paranoico/paranoica
paraplegic	el parapléjico/la parapléjica
parasite	el parásito
parasite infestation	la infestación del parásito
Parkinson's disease	la enfermedad de Parkinson
patch	el mechón, el parche
patella	la rótula
paternal	paterno/paterna
pathologist	el patólogo/la patóloga
patient	el/la paciente
pediatric	pediátrico/pediátrica
paediatrician	el/la pediatra
pediatrics	la pediatría
pelvic exam	el examen ginecológico
pelvic examination	el reconocimiento pélvico
pelvic inflamatory disease (PID)	la enfermedad inflamatoria pélvica

pelvis	la pelvis
penecillin	la penicilina
penile discharge	la secreción por el pene
penis	el pene
peptic ulcer	la úlcera péptica
perforation	la perforación
perianal abscess	el absceso perianal
perineum	el perineo
periodontal disease	la enfermedad
periodontal	
perspiration	la transpiración
pertussis	la tos ferina
Petri dish	la caja de Petri
pharmacist	el farmacéutico/la
farmacéutica	
pharmacy	la farmacia
pharynx	el faringe
phlegm	el escupo, la flema
phobia	la fobia
phosphorus	el fósforo
photosensitivity	la fotosensibilidad
physical examination	el examen físico
physical therapist	el/la terapeuta físico
physical therapy - PT	la terapia física
physician	el medico/la médica
physician's assistant	el/la asistente médico
profesional	
pill	la píldora, la pastilla
pillow	la almohada
pimples	los granitos
pinkeye	la conjuntivitis
pituitary gland	la glandula pituitaria
place of birth	el lugar de nacimiento
placenta	la placenta
plague	la plaga
plasma	el plasma
plastic surgeon	el cirujano plástico/la cirujana
plástica	
platelet	la plaqueta
pleurisy	la pleuresía
plozenge	la pastilla
pneumonia	la pulmonía
pocks	las marcas de viruelas
podiatrist	el/la podiatra
poison ivy	la hiedra venenosa
poison oak	el roble venenoso

poison sumac	el zumaque venenoso
poisoning	el envenenamiento
poisonous	venenoso/venenosa
police	la policía
polio	la poliomelitis
pollen	el polen
polyp	el pólipo
polyuria	la poliuria
poor circulation	la mala circulación
pore	el poro
postmenopausal	postmenopaúsico
postnatal care	el cuidado postnatal
post-op	después de la operación
postpartum	postparto
postpartum depression	la depresión posparto
potassium	el potasio
pound (weight)	la libra
powder	el polvo
predisposed	
predispuesto/predispuesta	
preeclampsia	la preeclampsia
pregnancy	el embarazo
pregnancy test	la prueba del embarazo
pregnant	embarazada
premature birth	el nacimiento prematuro
premenopausal	premenopáusico/premenopáusica
premenstrual syndrome - PMS	el síndrome premenstrual -SPM
prenatal care	el cuidado prenatal
presbyopia	la presbicia
prescription	la medicina de receta
pressure	la presión
prevention	la prevención
prickling	la comezón
primary care provider - PCP	el proveedor de atención primaria
private hospital room	la habitación privada
problems	los problemas
procedure	el procedimiento
proctologist	el/la proctólogo
proctology	la proctología
progesterone	la progesterona
prognosis	el pronóstico
prostate examination	el reconocimiento de la próstata
prostate gland	la próstata
prosthesis	la prótesis
prosthetic	protésico/protésica
protein	la proteína
psoriasis	la psoríasis

psychiatric hospital	el hospital psiquiátrico
psychiatrist	el/la psiquiatra
psychiatry	la psiquiatría
psychoanalysis	el psicoanálisis
psychologist	el psicólogo/la psicóloga
psychology	la psicología
psychosis	el psicosis
psychotherapy	la psicoterapia
psychotic	psicótico/psicótica
puberty	la pubertad
pubic lice	los piojos púbicos
puffy	inflado
pulled muscle	el músculo rasgado
pulmonary	pulmonar
pulmonary edema	el edema pulmonar
pulmonary function test	la prueba de función pulmonary
pulmonology	la neumología
pulsating	pulsativo/pulsativa
pulse	el pulso
pulse rate	la frequencia del pulso
pump	la bomba
puncture	el pinchazo
pupil	la pupila
purge	la purga
pus	el pus
pustule	la pustule
pyorrhea	la piorrea
pyuria	la piuria

Q

quadriceps	el cuádriceps
quarantine	la cuarentena
queasy	el propenso al vómito
question	la pregunta
quesy	
nauseabundo/nauseabunda	
quickly	rápidamente
quiet	silencioso/silenciosa
quinine	la quinina
quota	la cuota

R

rabies	la rabia
radiography	la radiografía
radiotherapy	la radioterapia
radiology	la radiología
rape	la violación
raped	violado(a)
rapid heartbeat	los latidos cardíacos rápidos
rashes	las erupciónes
Raynaud's phenomenon	el fenómeno de Raynaud
reaction	la reacción
receptionist	el/la recepcionista
recommendation	la recomendación
recommended dietary allowance (RDA)	la dosis diaria recomendada
record	el expediente
recovery room	la sala de recuperación
rectal exam	el tacto rectal
rectal prolapse	el prolapso del recto
recuperation	la recuperación
red blood cells	los glóbulos rojos
red blood count – RBC	el recuento de globulos rojos
redness	el enrojecimiento
referral	la recomendación
referred pain	el dolor referido
refill	el surtido nuevo
reflux	el reflujo
reflex	el reflejo
regurgitation	la regurgitación
relapse	la recaída
relaxed	relajado
relief	la ayuda, el alivio
remission	la remisión
removal	la extirpacion
renal failure	la insuficiencia renal
reproduction	la reproducción
reproductive organs	los órganos reproductivos
resection	la resección
resistance	la resistencia
respirator	el respirador
respiratory	respiratorio/respiratoria
restless legs	las piernas inquietas
result	el resultado
resuscitation	la resucitación
retardation	el retardo
retention	la retención
retina	la retina
retinitis	la retinitis
RH factor	el factor Rhesus/RH

rheumatic fever	la fiebre reumática
rheumatism	el reumatismo
rheumatoid arthritis	la artritis reumatoide
rheumatoid factor test	la prueba de factor reumatoide
rhinitis	la rinitis
rhinoplasty	la rinoplastia
rhythm method	el método del ritmo
rib cage	la caja toráxica
rickets	el raquitismo
right	la derecha
rigid	rígido/rígida
rigidity	la rigidez
rigor mortis	el rigor mortis
ringworm	la culebrilla
ringworm	la tiña
risk	el riesgo
risk factors	los factores de riesgo
root canal	el canal radicular
rosacea	la rosácea
roseola	la roséola
rub	la fricción
rubella	la rubéola
runny nose	la secreción nasal
rupture	la hernia, la ruptura

S

sacrum bones	los huesos del sacro
sad	triste
safe	seguro/segura
saline	salino/salina
saliva	la saliva
salmonella	la salmonella
salt	la sal
salve	la pomada
sample	la muestra
sane	cuerdo/cuerda
sanitary napkin	la toalla higiénica
sanity	la cordura
sarcoma	el sarcoma
satisfied	satisfecho/satisfecha
scab	la costra
scabies	la sarna
scald	la escaldadura
scale	la balanza

scalp	el cuero cabelludo
scalpel	el escalpelo
scaly	escamoso/escamosa
scapula	el omóplato
scar	la cicatriz
scared	espantado/espantada
scarlet fever	la fiebre escarlatina
scary	espantoso/espantosa
schizophrenia	la esquizofrenia
schizophrenic	esquizofrénico/esquizofrénica
sciatic	ciático/ciática
sciatica	la ciática
scissors	la tijeras
sclera	la esclerótica
scoliosis	la escoliosis
scorpion	el escorpión
scrape	el rasguño
scratch	el rasguño
scream	el grito
screen	el examen de detección
screening test	la prueba de detección
scrotum	el escroto
scurvy	el escorbuto
sealant	el sellante
seasickness	el mareo (en un barco)
secretion	la secreción
sedated	sedado
sedative	el sedante
sedentary	sedentario/sedentaria
seeing eye dog	el perro guía
seizures	los convulsiones
semen	el semen, la esperma
senile	senil
senility	la senilidad
sensation	la sensación
sensitive	sensible
sensitive to cold	friolento/friolenta
sensitivity	la sensibilidad
septum	el tabique
serious	serio/seria, grave
seriously ill	grave
serology	la serología
serum, I.V.	el suero
severe	severo/severa
sex	el sexo
sexual desire	el deseo sexual
sexual intercourse	la relacion sexual

sexual relations	las relaciones sexuales
sexuality	la sexualidad
sexually transmitted disease	la enfermedad de transmision
sexual	
sharp	filoso/filosa
sharp pain	el dolor agudo
shin	la espinilla
shingles	el herpes zoster
shiver	el escolafrío
shock	el choque
shortness of breath	la falta de respiración
shot	la inyección
shoulder	el hombro
shoulder blade	el omóplato
shower	la ducha
shunt	la desviación, el
cortocircuito	
siamese twins	los hermanos/las hermanas
siameses	
sibling	el hermano/la hermana
sick	enfermo/enferma
sickle cell anemia	la anemia de células
falciformes	
sickle cell disease	la enfermedad de células
falciformes	
sickly	el enfermizo/la enfermiza
side	el lado
side effect	el efecto secundario
siezure	la convulsión
sight	la visión
sigmoidoscopy	la sigmoidoscopia
simple fracture	la fractura simple
sinus	la cavidad hueca
sinus congestion	la congestión nasal
sinuses	los senos
sinusitis	la sinusitis
sitz-baths	los baños de asiento
skeleton	el esqueleto
skin	la piel
skin boil	el forúnculo
skin cancer	el cáncer de piel
skin discoloration	el paño
skin graft	el injerto cutáneo
skin infection	la infección de la piel
skinny	flaco/flaca
skull	el cráneo

sleep	el sueño
sleep apnea	la apnea del sueño
sleeping pill	el somnifero
sleeping sickness	la enfermedad del sueño
sleepless	sin sueño
sleepy	soñoliento/soñolienta
slight pain	el dolor leve
sling	el cabestrillo
slipped disk	el disco desplazado
small intestine	el intestino delgado
smallpox	la viruela
smell	el olor
smoke	el humo
smoking	el fumar tabaco
snack	la merienda
snakebite	la mordedura de serpiente
sneeze	el estornudo
snore	el ronquido
soap	el jabón
sober	sobrio/sobria
social worker	el trabajador/la trabajadora social
sodium	el sodio
soft	suave
sole (of the foot)	la planta del pie
sonogram	el sonograma
sore	dolorido/dolorida, la llaga
sore throat	el dolor de garganta
spasm	el espasmo
specialist	el/la especialista
specimen	el espécimen
spectacles	las gafas
speculum	el espéculo
speech	la habla
speech therapist	el/la terapeuta del habla
sperm	la semilla
spermicide	el espermecida
sphincter	el esfínter
spicy foods	los alimentos picantes
spider bite	la picadura de araña
spina bifida	la espina bífida
spinal column	la columna vertebral
spinal cord	la médula espinal
spinal fluid	el líquido cefalorraquídeo
spinal tap	la punción lumbar
spinal test	la prueba de la columna vertebral

spine	la columna vertebral
spirometry	la espirometria
spleen	el bazo
splint	la férula
splinter	la astilla
sponge	la esponja
spots	las manchas
spotted fever	la fiebre púrpura
sprain	la torcedura
spray nasal	el spray nasal
sputum	el esputo
squint	el estrabismo
stab	la puñalada
stable	estable
starvation	la inanición
sterile	estéril
sterility	la esterilidad
sterilization	la esterilización
sternum	el esternón
steroid	la esteroide
stethoscope	el estetoscopio
stiff	rígido/rígida
stiff neck	el cuello rígido
stillbirth	la muerte fetal
stillborn	el nacido muerto
stimulant	la estimulante
sting	la picadura
stirrup	el estribo
stitch	la puntada
stitches	los puntos de suturas
stoma	el estoma
stomach	el estómago
stomach ache	el dolor del estómago
stomach gas	el gas en el estomago
stomach pain	el dolor del estómago
stomach ulcer	la úlcera del estómago
stomach virus	el virus de estómago
stool	las heces, el excremento
stool softener	el ablandador fecal
stool specimen	la muestra de heces
straight jacket	la camisa de fuerza
strain	la tensión
strength	la fuerza
streptococcal infection	la infección estreptocóccica
stress	el estrés
stress test	la prueba de esfuerzo

stretch mark	la estría
stretcher	la camilla
stroke	el derrame cerebral
stroller	el cochecillo
strong	fuerte
stuffy nose	la nariz tapada
stupor	el estupor
stuttering	el tartamudeo, tartamudo
sty	el orzuelo
suffocation	la sofocación
suicide	el suicidio
sunburn	la quemadura por el sol
sunscreen	el filtro solar
sunstroke	la insolación
supplement	el suplemento
suppository	el supositorio
surgeon	el cirujano/la cirujana
surgery	la cirugía
surgical	quirúrgico/quirúrgica
surgical procedure quirúrgico	el procedimiento
surrogate mother	la madre subrogada
susceptible	susceptible
suture la	sutura
swelling inflamación	la hinchazón, la
swollen	hinchado/hinchada
swollen glands	los ganglios inflamados
symptomatic	sintomática
symptoms	los síntomas
syndrome	el síndrome
synthetic	sintético/sintética
synthetic thyroid hormone	la hormona tiroidea sintética
syphilis	la sífilis
syringe	la jeringa
syrup	el jarabe

T

---

table	la mesa
tablespoon	la cucharada
tablet	la pastilla
tailbone	el cóccix
talcum powder	el talco
tampon	el tampón
tapeworm	la tenia

tartar	el sarro
taste	el sabor, el gusto
taste bud	la papila gustativa
tattoo	el tatuaje
tear	la lágrima
tear duct	el conducto lacrimar
teaspoon	la cucharadita
technician	el técnico/la técnica
teething	la dentición
temperature	la temperatura
temple (of the head)	la sien
temporary	temporal
temporary	transitorio/transitoria
tender	adolorido
tendon	el tendón
tendonitis	la tendinitis
tennis elbow	el codo de tenista
terminal	terminal
test	el examen, la prueba
test strip	la tira de prueba
test tube	la probeta
testicles	los testículos
testosterone	la testosterona
tetanus	el tétano
tetanus shot la inyección	contra el tétano
therapeutic abortion	el aborto terapéutico
therapist	el/la terapeuta
therapy	la terapia
thermometer	el termómetro
thick	grueso/gruesa,
espeso/espesa	
thigh	el muslo
thin	delgado/delgada,
fino/fina	
thirst	la sed
thorax	el tórax
throat	la garganta
throat culture	el cultivo de la garganta
throb	el latido
throbbing	pulsante
thrombosis	la trombosis
thumb	el pulgar
thyroid	la tiroides
thyroid gland	la glándula tiroides
tic	el tic
tick	la garrapata

147

tick bite	la mordedura de garrapata
tincture	la tintura
tingling	el hormigueo
tinnitus	el tinitus
tired	cansado/cansada
tiredness	la fatiga
tissue	el tejido
tissue paper	el pañuelo de papel
to admit	internar
to adopt	adoptar
to advise	aconsejar
to amputate	amputar
to atrophy	atrofiarse
to avoid	evitar
to bathe	bañar(se)
to be admitted	ser internado/internada
to be anxious	tener ansias
to be born	nacer
to be congested	estar congestionado
to be constipated	estar estreñido
to be depressed	estar deprimido
to be nervous	estar nervioso
to be sad	tener tristeza
to be sleepy	tener sueño
to be thirsty	tener sed
to be vomiting	tener vómitos
to become dizzy	marearse
to bleed	sangrar
to blink	parpadear
to bother	molestar
to break	quebrar, romper
to break water	romper la bolsa de agua
to breastfeed	lactar
to breathe	respirar
to burp	eructar
to catheterize	cateterizar
to chew	masticar
to choke	ahogar(se)
to circumcise	circuncidar
to commit suicide	suicidarse
to conceive	concebir
to consent	consentir
to consult	consultar
to cough	toser
to crawl	gatear
to cripple	lisiar
to crush	moler

to cry	llorar
to cure	curar
to cut	cortar
to defecate	defecar
to deliver a baby	parir
to develop	desarollar
to diagnose	diagnosticar
to die	morir
to digest	digerir
to dilute	diluir
to discharge	dar de alta
to discontinue	descontinuar
to disfigure	desfigurar
to disinfect	desinfectar
to dislocate	zafar
to distend	distender(se)
to drain	supurar
to draw blood	sacar sangre
to drink	beber
to drown	ahogar(se)
to eat	comer
to ejaculate	eyacular
to elevate	elevar
to examine	examinar
to exercise	hacer ejercicio
to exhale	exhalar
to explain	explicar
to extract	extraer
to faint	desmayar(se)
to fall	caer(se)
to fast	ayunar
to feed	alimentar, dar de comer
to feel	sentir(se)
to fight	pelear
to fill in	despachar
to finish	terminar
to freeze	congelar
to function	funcionar
to gag	sentir náusea(s)
to gain weight	engordar
to gargle	gargarizar
to get well	componer
to give	dar
to give birth to	dar a luz
to grieve	afligirse
to grind	moler

to harm	dañar
to heal	curarse
to hear	oír
to help	ayudar
to hemorrhage	sangrar
to hospitalize	ingresar
to hurt	doler
to hydrate	hidratar
to immunize	inmunizar
to implant	implantar
to improve	mejorar
to induce	inducir
to infect	infectar
to ingest	ingerir
to inhale	inhalar
to inject	inyectar
to injure	herir, lastimar
to inoculate	inocular
to insert	insertar
to irrigate	irrigar
to isolate	aislar
to itch	sentir picazón
to kill	matar
to lactate	lactar
to limp	cojear
to lipread	leer los labios
to listen	escuchar
to live	vivir
to lose consciousness	perder el conocimiento
to lubricate	lubricar, mojar
to massage	masajear
to medicate	dar medicina
to medicate	medicinar
to menstruate	menstruar
to metabolize	metabolizar
to molest	molestar
to monitor	monitorear
to mourn	llorar
to name	nombrar
to need	necesitar
to nurture	nutrir, criar
to operate	operar
to ovulate	ovular
to pant	jadear
to pass gas	pasar gas
to penetrate	penetrar
to perspire	transpirar

to poison	envenenar
to practice	ensayar
to predispose	predisponer
to prescribe	recetar
to prevent	prevenir
to prick	picar
to push	pujar
to quarantine	poner en cuarentena
to quit	renunciar
to recommend	recomendar
to reconstruct	reconstruir
to recover	curarse
to recuperate	recuperarse
to refill	rellenar, surtir
to rehabilitate	rehabilitar
to rehydrate	rehidratar
to reject	rechazar
to remove	quitar(se)
to replace	reemplazar
to replicate	replicar
to reproduce	reproducir
to rest	descansar
to resuscitate	resucitar
to revive	reanimar(se), revivir
to rub	frotar
to screen	practicar exámenes de detección
to secrete	secretar
to see	ver
to shave	afeitar(se)
to shiver	estremecerse
to shower	ducharse
to sleep	dormir
to sleepwalk	caminar dormido
to slip	resbalar
to slur	arrastrar las palabras
to smell	oler
to smoke	fumar
to sneeze	estornudar
to snore	roncar
to spit	escupir
to splint	entablillar
to sprain	torcer(se)
to stain	manchar
to stand	ponerse de pie
to sterilize	esterilizar

to sting	picar
to stitch	suturar
to stitch up	coser
to strain	colar
to strangle	estrangular(se)
to stutter	tartamudear
to suffer	sufrir
to support	apoyar
to survive	sobrevivir
to suture	suturar
to swallow	tragar
to swell	hinchar
to take	tomar
to take out	sacar
to test	probar
to throw up	devolver, vomitar
to tie tubes	ligar las trompas
to tolerate	tolerar
to touch	tocar
to transplant	trasplantar
to treat	tratar
to upset	trastornar
to urinate	orinar
to use	usar
to vaccinate	vacunar
to visit	visita
to vomit	deponer
to wake up	despertarse, despertar
to walk	caminar
to wash	lavar
to wean	destetar
to weigh	pesar
to wheeze	respirar con chiflidos
to yawn	bostezar
toadstool	los hongos venenosos
tobacco	el tabaco
toe	el dedo del pie
toilet	el inodoro
tongue	la lengua
tongue depressor	el depresor de lengua
tonic	el tónico
tonsil	la amígdala
tonsilitis	la tonsilitis
tonsillectomy	la tonsilectomía
tooth	el diente
toothache	el dolor de dientes
toothbrush	el cepillo de dientes

toothpaste	la pasta de dientes
torn ligament	el ligamento desgarrado
touch	el tacto
tourniquet	el torniquete, la ligadura
towel	la toalla
toxemia	la toxemia
toxic	tóxico/tóxica
toxin	la toxina
traces	las trazas
trachea	la tráquea
traction	la tracción
tranquilizer	el tranquilizante, el calmante
transfusion	la transfusión
transmitted	transmitido/transmitida
transplant	el trasplante
trauma	el trauma, el traumatismo
traumatic	traumático/traumática
treatment	el tratamiento
treatment plan	el plan de tratamiento
tremors	los tremores
triceps	el tríceps
trichomonas	las tricomonas
trimester	el trimestre
trouble	la molestia
tubal ligation	la ligadura de trompas
tubal pregnancy	el embarazo tubarico
tubal rupture	la rotura de trompas
tube	la trompa
tuberculin test	la prueba de tuberculina
tuberculosis - TB	la tuberculosis
tumor	el tumor
tunnel vision	la vision del tunel
tweezers	las pinzas
twin	el gemelo/la gemela
twisted	torcido/torcida
typhoid fever	la fiebre tifoidea
typhus	el tifus

U

ulcer	la úlcera
ultrasound	el ultrasonido
ultraviolet treatment - UVA	el tratamiento untravioleta
umbilical cord	el cordón umbilical

uncomfortable	incómodo/incómoda
unconscious	inconsciente
unconsciousness	la pérdida del conocimiento
undernourished	subnutridos, desnutridas
unhappy	infeliz
unhealthy	insalubre
unstable	inestable
unusual	raro/rara
upset	trastornado/transtornada
upset stomach	la molestia estomacal
uremia	la uremia
urethra	la urétra
urgent	urgente
uric acid	el ácido úrico
urinal	el orinal
urinalysis	el análisis de orina
urinary	urinario/urinaria
urinary pain	el dolor cuando orina
urinary tract infection	la infección de la orina
urinary urgency	la urgencia urinaria
urine	la orina
urine sample	la muestra de orina
urologist	el urólogo/la uróloga
urology	la urología
uterine cramps	las calambres uterinos
uterine pain	el dolor de útero
uterine rupture	la ruptura uterine
uterus	el útero
uvula	la uvula

V

vaccination	la vacunación
vaccine	la vacuna
vagina la	vagina
vaginal	vaginal
vaginal bleeding	el sangrado vaginal
vaginal discharge	el flujo de la vagina
vaginal dryness	la sequedad vaginal
vaginal lubricant	el lubricante vaginal
vaginitis	la vaginitis
valve	la válvula
varicose vein	la vena varicosa
vascular	vascular
vasectomy	la vasectomía

vegetative	vegetativo/vegatativa
vein	la vena
venereal diseases	las enfermedades venéreas
venom	el veneno
ventilator	el ventilador
ventricle	el ventrículo
vertebrae	las vértebras
vertigo	el vértigo
victim	la víctima
viral	viral
virile	viril
virus	el virus
vision	la visión, la vista
vision test	el examen de la vista
visual changes	los cambios visuales
vital	vital
vital organ	el órgano vital
vital signs	los signos vitales
vitamin	la vitamina
vocal cord	la cuerda vocal
voice	la voz
volvulus	el vólvulo
vomit	el vómito
vomiting	estar vomitando

W

waist	el talle
waiting room	la sala de espera
walker	el andador
ward	la sala
warning	el aviso
wart	la verruga
water	el agua
watery eyes	los ojos llorosos
weak	débil
weakness	la debilidad
weary	fatigado/fatigada
weather	el tiempo
weight	el peso
weight change	el cambio de peso
weight loss	la pérdida de peso
welfare	la bienestar (asistencia social)
welt	el verdugón

wet nurse	la nodriza
wheelchair	la silla de ruedas
wheezing	la sibilancia
whiplash	la lesión de latigazo
whistle	el silbido
white blood cells	las células blancas de sangre
white blood cells	los glóbulos blancos
white blood count - WBC	el recuento de globulos blancos
whooping cough	la tos ferina
wig	la peluca
will power	la fuerza de voluntad
windpipe	el gaznate
wisdom tooth	la muela del juicio
withdrawal	la retirada
woman	la mujer
womb	la matriz
worried	preocupado/preocupada
worse	peor
wound	la herida
wounded	herido/herida
wrist	la muñeca

X

xenophobia	la xenofobia
x-ray technician	el técnico/la tecnica de radiografía
x-rays	las radiografías

Y

yawn	el bostezo
yearly	anualmente
yeast infection	la infccción por hongos
yellow fever	la fiebre amarilla
yellow skin	la piel amarilla

Conclusion

I hope this book was able to help you learn medical Spanish and empower you to communicate effectively and confidently with your patients and fellow professionals.

The next step is to apply your communication skills in a cross-cultural environment.

Made in the USA
Middletown, DE
13 April 2018